Hiroshima

John Hersey

HIROSHIMA

PUBLISHERS' NOTE

ON Monday, August 6th, 1945, a new era in human history opened. After years of intensive research and experiment, conducted in their later stages mainly in America, by scientists of many nationalities, Japanese among them, the forces which hold together the constituent particles of the atom had at last been harnessed to man's use: and on that day man used them. By a decision of the American military authorities, made, it is said, in defiance of the protests of many of the scientists who had worked on the project, an atomic bomb was dropped on Hiroshima. As a direct result, some 60,000 Japanese men, women and children were killed, and 100,000 injured; and almost the whole of a great seaport, a city of 250,000 people, was destroyed by blast or by fire. As an indirect result, a few days later, Japan acknowledged defeat, and the Second World War came to an end.

For many months little exact and reliable news about the details of the destruction wrought by the first atomic bomb reached Western readers. Millions of words were written, in Europe and America, explaining the marvellous new powers that science had placed in men's hands; describing the researches and experiments that had led up to this greatest of all disclosures of Nature's secrets: discussing the problems for man's future which the new weapon raised. Argument waxed furious as to the ethics of the bomb: should the Japanese have received advance warning of America's intention to use it? Should a demonstration bomb have been exploded in the presence of enemy observers in some remote spot where it would do a minimum of damage, as a warning to the Japanese people, before its first serious use? But of the feelings and reactions of the people of Hiroshima to the bomb, nothing, or at least nothing that was not pure imagination, could be written; for nothing was known.

In May, 1946, *The New Yorker* sent John Hersey, journalist and author of *A Bell for Adano*, to the Far East to find out what had really happened at Hiroshima: to interview survivors of the catastrophe, to endeavour to describe what they had seen and felt and thought, what the destruction of their city, their lives and homes and hopes and friends, had meant to them—in short, the cost of the bomb in terms of human suffering and reaction to suffering. He stayed in Japan for a month, gathering his own material with little, if any, help from the occupying authorities; he obtained the stories from actual witnesses. The characters in his account are living individuals, not composite types. The story is their own story, told as far as possible in their own words. On August 31st, 1946, Hersey's story was made public. For the first time in *The New Yorker's* career an issue appeared which, within the familiar covers, bearing—for such covers are prepared long in advance—a picnic scene, carried no satire, no cartoons, no fiction, no verse or smart quips or shopping notes: nothing but its advertisement matter and Hersey's 30,000-word story.

That story is built round the experiences of six people who were in Hiroshima when the bomb dropped, each of whom, by some strange chance, escaped, not unscathed, but at least with life. One, a Roman Catholic missionary priest, was a German; the other five were Japanese: a Red Cross hospital doctor, another doctor with a private practice, an office girl, a Protestant clergyman, and a tailor's widow. For some time after the bomb had fallen, none of them knew exactly what had happened: they hardly realised that their old familiar life had ended, that they had been chosen by chance, or destiny, or—as two of them at any rate would have put it—by God, to be helpless small-part actors in an unparalleled tragedy. Bit by bit came the awakening to the magnitude of the calamity that had removed, in a flash, nearly all their accustomed world.

Hersey's vivid yet matter-of-fact story tells what the bomb did to each of these six people, through the hours and the days that followed its impact on their lives. It is written soberly, with no attempt whatever to "pile on the agony"—the presentation at times is almost cold in its economy of words. To six ordinary men and women, at the time and afterwards, it seemed —like this.

The New Yorker's original intention was to make the story a serial. But in an inspired moment, the paper's editors saw that it must be published as a single whole and decided to devote a whole issue to Hersey's masterpiece of reconstruction. For ten days Hersey feverishly rewrote and polished his story, handing it out by instalments to the printers, and no hint of what was in the air escaped from *The New Yorker* office. On August 31st, in the paper's usual format, the historic issue appeared. It created a first-order sensation in American journalistic history : a few hours after publication the issue was sold out. Applications poured in for permission to serialise the story in other American journals, among them the New York *Herald Tribune*, Washington *Post*, Chicago *Sun*, and Boston *Globe*. A condensed version—the cuts personally approved by Hersey—was broadcast in four instalments by the American Broadcasting Company. Some fifty newspapers in the U.S. eventually obtained permission to use the story in serial form, the copyright fees, after tax deduction, at Hersey's direction going to the American Red Cross. Albert Einstein ordered a thousand copies of the *New Yorker* containing the story. Even stage rights were sought from the author, though he refused to give permission for dramatisation. British newspapers and press syndicates immediately cabled for reproduction rights : but the *New Yorker's* executives insisted that no cutting could be permitted, and with British paper rationing, full newspaper publication was seen to be impracticable. The book production rights for the United States were secured by Alfred A. Knopf, Inc., and the American Book of the Month Club chose it for publication as an "Extra" ; and the B.B.C. obtained permission to broadcast the article in full in four episodes as part of their new Third Programme.

Penguin Books, feeling that Hersey's story should receive the widest possible circulation in Great Britain, immediately cabled to Alfred A. Knopf for, and were accorded, permission to issue it complete in book form. It here appears—save for following English spelling conventions—in an edition of 250,000 copies, exactly as it appeared in the pages of the *New Yorker*.

Many accounts have been published telling—so far as security considerations allow—*how* the atom bomb works. But here, for the first time, is not a description of scientific triumphs, of intricate machines, new elements, and mathematical formulas, but an account of *what* the bomb does—seen through the eyes of some of those to whom it did it: of those who endured one of the world's most catastrophic experiences, and lived.

HIROSHIMA

The following note
appeared in the NEW YORKER *of 31 August, 1946.*
as an introduction to John Hersey's article

The NEW YORKER this week devotes its entire editorial space to an article on the almost complete obliteration of a city by one atomic bomb, and what happened to the people of that city. It does so in the conviction that few of us have yet comprehended the all but incredible destructive power of this weapon, and that everyone might well take time to consider the terrible implications of its use.

I.

A NOISELESS FLASH

AT exactly fifteen minutes past eight in the morning, on August 6th, 1945, Japanese time, at the moment when the atomic bomb flashed above Hiroshima, Miss Toshiko Sasaki, a clerk in the personnel department at the East Asia Tin Works, had just sat down at her place in the plant office and was turning her head to speak to the girl at the next desk. At that same moment, Dr. Masakazu Fujii was settling down cross-legged to read the Osaka *Asahi* on the porch of his private hospital, overhanging one of the seven deltaic rivers which divide Hiroshima; Mrs. Hatsuyo Nakamura, a tailor's widow, stood by the window of her kitchen watching a neighbour tearing down his house because it lay in the path of an air-raid-defence fire lane; Father Wilhelm Kleinsorge, a German priest of the Society of Jesus, reclined in his underwear on a cot on the top floor of his order's three-storey mission house, reading a Jesuit magazine, *Stimmen der Zeit*; Dr. Terufumi Sasaki, a young member of the surgical staff of the city's large, modern Red Cross Hospital, walked along one of the hospital corridors with a blood specimen for a Wassermann test in his hand; and the Reverend Mr. Kiyoshi Tanimoto, pastor of the Hiroshima Methodist Church, paused at the door of a rich man's house in Koi, the city's western suburb, and prepared to unload a handcart full of things he·had evacuated from town in fear of the massive B29 raid which everyone expected Hiroshima to suffer. A hundred thousand people were killed

by the atomic bomb, and these six were among the
survivors. They still wonder why they lived when so
many others died. Each of them counts many small
items of chance or volition—a step taken in time, a
decision to go indoors, catching one street-car instead
of the next—that spared him. And now each knows
that in the act of survival he lived a dozen lives and saw
more death than he ever thought he would see. At the
time none of them knew anything.

The Reverend Mr. Tanimoto got up at five o'clock
that morning. He was alone in the parsonage, because
for some time his wife had been commuting with their
year-old baby to spend nights with a friend in Ushida,
a suburb to the north. Of all the important cities of
Japan, only two, Kyoto and Hiroshima, had not been
visited in strength by *B-san*, or Mr. B, as the Japanese
with a mixture of respect and unhappy familiarity,
called the B-29; and Mr. Tanimoto, like all his neighbours and friends, was almost sick with anxiety. He
had heard uncomfortably detailed accounts of mass
raids on Kure, Iwakuni, Tokuyama, and other nearby
towns; he was sure Hiroshima's turn would come
soon. He had slept badly the night before, because
there had been several air-raid warnings. Hiroshima
had been getting such warnings almost every night for
weeks, for at that time the B-29s were using Lake Biwa,
north-east of Hiroshima, as a rendezvous point, and no
matter what city the Americans planned to hit, the
Super-fortresses streamed in over the coast near
Hiroshima. The frequency of the warnings and the
continued abstinence of Mr. B with respect to Hiroshima had made its citizens jittery; a rumour was going

around that the Americans were saving something special for the city.

Mr. Tanimoto is a small man, quick to talk, laugh, and cry. He wears his black hair parted in the middle and rather long; the prominence of the frontal bones just above his eyebrows and the smallness of his moustache, mouth, and chin give him a strange, old-young look, boyish and yet wise, weak and yet fiery. He moves nervously and fast, but with a restraint which suggests that he is a cautious, thoughtful man. He showed, indeed, just those qualities in the uneasy days before the bomb fell. Besides having his wife spend the nights in Ushida, Mr. Tanimoto had been carrying all the portable things from his church, in the close-packed residential district called Nagaragawa, to a house that belonged to a rayon manufacturer in Koi, two miles from the centre of town. The rayon man, a Mr. Matsui, had opened his then unoccupied estate to a large number of his friends and acquaintances, so that they might evacuate whatever they wished to a safe distance from the probable target area. Mr. Tanimoto had no difficulty in moving chairs, hymnals, Bibles, altar gear, and church records by pushcart himself, but the organ console and an upright piano required some aid. A friend of his named Matsuo had, the day before, helped him get the piano out to Koi; in return, he had promised this day to assist Mr. Matsuo in hauling out a daughter's belongings. That is why he had risen so early.

Mr. Tanimoto cooked his own breakfast. He felt awfully tired. The effort of moving the piano the day before, a sleepless night, weeks of worry and unbalanced diet, the cares of his parish—all combined to make him feel hardly adequate to the new day's work. There was another thing, too: Mr. Tanimoto had studied theology at Emory College, in Atlanta, Georgia; he had graduated in 1940; he spoke excellent English; he dressed in American clothes; he had corresponded with many American friends right up to the time the 'war began; and among a people obsessed with a fear of being spied upon—perhaps almost obsessed himself—he found himself growing increasingly uneasy. The police had questioned him several times, and just a few days before, he had heard that an influential acquaintance, a Mr. Tanaka, a retired officer of the Toyo Kisen Kaisha steamship line, an anti-Christian, a man famous in Hiroshima for his showy philanthropies and notorious for his personal tyrannies, had been telling people that Tanimoto should not be trusted. In compensation, to show himself publicly a good Japanese, Mr. Tanimoto had taken on the chairmanship of his local *tonarigumi*, or Neighbourhood Association, and to his other duties and concerns this position had added the business of organising air-raid defence for about twenty families.

Before six o'clock that morning, Mr. Tanimoto started for Mr. Matsuo's house. There he found that their burden was to be a *tansu*, a large Japanese cabinet, full of clothing and household goods. The two men, set out. The morning was perfectly clear and so warm that the day promised to be uncomfortable. A few. minutes after they started, the air raid siren went off— a minute-long blast that warned of approaching planes but indicated to the people of Hiroshima only a slight degree of danger, since it sounded every morning at this time, when an American weather plane came over. The two men pulled and pushed the handcart through the city streets. Hiroshima was a fan-shaped city, lying mostly on the six islands formed by the seven estuarial rivers that branch out from the Ota River; its main commercial and residential districts, covering about four square miles in the centre of the city, contained three-quarters of its population, which had been reduced by several evacuation programmes from a wartime peak of 380,000 to about 245,000. Factories and other residential districts, or suburbs, lay compactly around the edges of the city. To the south were the docks, an airport, and an island-studded Inland Sea. A rim of mountains runs around the other three sides of the delta. Mr. Tanimoto and Mr. Matsuo took their way through the shopping centre, already full of people, and across two of the rivers to the sloping streets of Koi, and up them to the outskirts and foot-hills. As they started up a valley away from the tight-ranked houses, the all-clear sounded. (The Japanese radar operators, detecting only three planes, supposed that they comprised a reconnaissance.) Pushing the handcart up to the rayon man's house was tiring, and the men, after they had manoeuvred their load into the driveway and to the front steps, paused to rest awhile. They stood with a wing of the house between them and the city. Like most homes in this part of Japan, the house consisted of a wooden frame and wooden walls supporting a heavy tile roof. Its front hall, packed with rolls of bedding and clothing, looked like a cool cave full of fat cushions. Opposite the house, to the right of the front door, there was a large, finicky rock garden. There was no sound of planes. The morning was still; the place was cool and pleasant.

Then a tremendous flash of light cut across the sky. Mr. Tanimoto has a distinct recollection that it travelled from east to west, from the city toward the hills. It seemed a sheet of sun. Both he and Mr. Matsuo reacted in terror—and both had time to react (for they were 3,500 yards, or two miles, from the centre of the explosion). Mr. Matsuo dashed up the front steps into the house and dived among the bedrolls and buried himself there. Mr. Tanimoto took four or five steps and threw himself between two big rocks in the garden. He bellied up very hard against one of them. As his face was against the stone he did not see what happened. He felt a sudden pressure, and then splinters and pieces of board and fragments of tile fell on him. He heard no roar. (Almost no one in Hiroshima recalls hearing any noise of the bomb. But a fisherman in his sampan on the Inland Sea near Tsuzu, the man with whom Mr. Tanimoto's mother-in-law and sister-in-law were living, saw the flash and heard a tremendous explosion; he was nearly twenty miles from Hiroshima, but the thunder was greater than when the B-29s hit Iwakuni, only five miles away.)

When he dared, Mr. Tanimoto raised his head and saw that the rayon man's house had collapsed. He thought a bomb had fallen directly on it. Such clouds of dust had risen that there was a sort of twilight around. In panic, not thinking for the moment of Mr. Matsuo under the ruins, he dashed out into the

street. He noticed as he ran that the concrete wall of
the estate had fallen over—toward the house rather
than away from it. In the street, the first thing he
saw was a squad of soldiers who had been burrowing
into the hillside opposite, making one of the thousands
of dugouts in which the Japanese apparently intended
to resist invasion, hill by hill, life for life; the soldiers
were coming out of the hole, where they should have
been safe, and blood was running from their heads,
chests and backs. They were silent and dazed.

Under what seemed to be a local dust cloud, the day
grew darker and darker.

At nearly midnight, the night before the bomb was
dropped, an announcer on the city's radio station said
that about two hundred B-29s were approaching
southern Honshū and advised the population of
Hiroshima to evacuate to their designated " safe
areas." Mrs. Hatsuyo Nakamura, the tailor's widow
who lived in the section called Nobori-cho and who had
long had a habit of doing as she was told, got her three
children—a ten-year-old boy, Toshio, an eight-year-old
girl, Yaeko, and a five-year-old girl, Myeko—out of
bed and dressed them and walked with them to the
military area known as the East Parade Ground, on
the north-east edge of the city. There she unrolled
some mats and the children lay down on them. They
slept until about two, when they were awakened by the
roar of the planes going over Hiroshima. As soon as
the planes had passed, Mrs. Nakamura started back
with her children. They reached home a little after
two-thirty and she immediately turned on the radio,
which, to her distress, was just then broadcasting a

fresh warning. When she looked at the children and saw how tired they were, and when she thought of the number of trips they had made in past weeks, all to no purpose, to the East Parade Ground, she decided that in spite of the instructions on the radio, she simply could not face starting out all over again. She put the children in their bedrolls on the floor, lay down herself at three o'clock, and fell asleep at once, so soundly that when planes passed over later, she did not waken to their sound.

The siren jarred her awake at about seven. She arose, dressed quickly, and hurried to the house of Mr. Nakamoto, the head of her Neighbourhood Association, and asked him what she should do. He said that she should remain at home unless an urgent warning—a series of intermittent blasts of the siren— was sounded. She returned home, lit the stove in the kitchen, set some rice to cook, and sat down to read that morning's Hiroshima *Chugoku*. To her relief, the all-clear sounded at eight o'clock. She heard the children stirring, so she went and gave each of them a handful of peanuts and told them to stay on their bedrolls, because they were tired from the night's walk. She had hoped that they would go back to sleep, but the man in the house directly to the south began to make a terrible hullabaloo of hammering, wedging, ripping, and splitting. The prefectural government, convinced, as everyone in Hiroshima was, that the city would be attacked soon, had began to press with threats and warnings for the completion of wide fire lanes, which, it' was hoped, might act in conjunction with the rivers to localise any fires started by an incendiary raid; and the neighbour was reluctantly sacrificing his home to the city's safety. Just the day before, the prefecture had ordered all able-bodied girls from the secondary schools to spend a few days helping to clear these lanes, and they started work soon after the all-clear sounded.

Mrs. Nakamura went back to the kitchen, looked at the rice, and began watching the man next door. At first she was annoyed with him for making so much noise, but then she was moved almost to tears by pity. Her emotion was specifically directed toward her neighbour, tearing down his home, board by board, at a time when there was so much unavoidable destruction, but undoubtedly she also felt a generalised, community pity, to say nothing of self-pity. She had not had an easy time. Her husband, Isawa, had gone into the army just after Myeko was born, and she had heard nothing from or of him for a long time, until, on March 5th, 1942, she received a seven-word telegram: "Isawa died an honourable death at Singapore." She learned later that he had died on February 15th, the day Singapore fell, and that he had been a corporal. Isawa had not been a particularly prosperous tailor, and his only capital was a Sankoku sewing machine. After his death, when his allotments stopped coming, Mrs. Nakamuru got out the machine and began to take in piecework herself, and since then had supported the children, but poorly, by sewing.

As Mrs. Nakamura stood watching her neighbour, everything flashed whiter than any white she had ever seen. She did not notice what happened to the man next door; the reflex of a mother set her in motion toward her children. She had taken a single step (the house was 1,350 yards, or three-quarters of a mile, from the centre of the explosion) when something picked her up and she seemed to fly into the next room over the raised sleeping platform, pursued by parts of her house.

Timbers fell around her as she landed, and a shower of tiles pommelled her; everything became dark, for she was buried. The debris did not cover her deeply. She rose up and freed herself. She heard a child cry, " Mother, help me ! " and saw her youngest— Myeko, the five-year-old—buried up to her breast and unable to move. As Mrs. Nakamura started frantically to claw her way toward the baby, she could see or hear nothing of her other children.

In the days right before the bombing, Dr. Masakazu Fujii, being prosperous, hedonistic, and, at the time not too busy, had been allowing himself the luxury of sleeping until nine or nine-thirty, but fortunately he had to get up early the morning the bomb was dropped to see a house guest off on a train. He rose at six, and half an hour later walked with his friend to the station, not far away, across two of the rivers. He was back home by seven, just as the siren sounded its sustained warning. He ate breakfast and then, because the morning was already hot, undressed down to his underwear and went out on the porch to read the paper. This porch—in fact, the whole building— was curiously constructed. Dr. Fujii was the proprietor of a peculiarly Japanese institution, a private, single-doctor hospital. This building, perched beside and over the water of the Kyo River, and next to the bridge of the same name, contained thirty rooms for thirty patients and their kinsfolk—for, according to Japanese custom, when a person falls sick and goes to a hospital, one or more members of his family go and live there with him, to cook for him, bathe, massage, and read to him, and to offer incessant familial sympathy, without which a Japanese patient would be miserable indeed. Dr. Fujii had no beds—only straw mats—for his patients. He did, however, have all sorts of modern equipment: an X-ray machine, diathermy apparatus, and a fine tiled laboratory. The structure rested two-thirds on the land, one-third on piles over the tidal waters of the Kyo. This overhang, the part of the building where Dr. Fujii lived, was queer-looking, but it was cool in summer and from the porch, which faced away from the centre of the city, the prospect of the river, with pleasure boats drifting up and down it, was always refreshing. Dr. Fujii had occasionally had anxious moments when the Ota and its mouth branches rose to flood, but the piling was apparently firm enough and the house had always held.

Dr. Fujii had been relatively idle for about a month because in July, as the number of untouched cities in Japan dwindled and as Hiroshima seemed more and more inevitably a target, he began turning patients away, on the ground that in case of a fire raid he would not be able to evacuate them. Now he had only two patients left—a woman from Yano, injured in the shoulder, and a young man of twenty-five recovering from burns he had suffered when the steel factory near Hiroshima in which he worked had been hit. Dr. Fujii had six nurses to tend his patients. His wife and

children were safe; his wife and one son were living
outside Osaka, and another son and two daughters
were in the country on Kyushu. A niece was living
with him, and a maid and a manservant. He had little
to do and did not mind, for he had saved some money.
At fifty he was healthy, convivial, and calm, and he was
pleased to pass the evenings drinking whisky with
friends, always sensibly and for the sake of conversation. Before the war, he had affected brands imported
from Scotland and America; now he was perfectly
satisfied with the best Japanese brand, Suntory.

Dr. Fujii sat down cross-legged in his underwear on
the spotless matting of the porch, put on his glasses,
and started reading the Osaka *Asahi*. He liked to read
the Osaka news because his wife was there. He saw
the flash. To him—faced away from the centre and
looking at his paper—it seemed a brilliant yellow.
Startled, he began to rise to his feet. In that moment
(he was 1,550 yards from the centre), the hospital leaned
behind his rising and, with a terrible ripping noise,
toppled into the river. The Doctor, still in the act of
getting to his feet, was thrown forward and around and
over; he was buffetted and gripped; he lost track of
everything, because things were so speeded up; he felt
the water.

Dr. Fujii hardly had time to think that he was dying
before he realized that he was alive, squeezed tightly
by two long timbers in a V across his chest, like a
morsel suspended between two huge chopsticks—held
upright, so that he could not move, with his head
miraculously above water and his torso and legs in it.
The remains of his hospital were all around him in a

mad assortment of splintered lumber and materials for the relief of pain. His left shoulder hurt terribly. His glasses were gone.

Father Wilhelm Kleinsorge, of the Society of Jesus, was, on the morning of the explosion, in rather frail condition. The Japanese war-time diet had not sustained him, and he felt the strain of being a foreigner in an increasingly xenophobic Japan; even a German, since the defeat of the Fatherland, was unpopular. Father Kleinsorge had, at thirty-eight, the look of a boy growing too fast—thin in the face, with a prominent Adam's apple, a hollow chest, dangling hands, big feet. He walked clumsily, leaning forward a little. He was tired all the time. To make matters worse, he had suffered for two days, along with Father Cieslik, a fellow-priest, from a rather painful and urgent diarrhoea, which they blamed on the beans and black ration bread they were obliged to eat. Two other priests then living in the mission compound, which was in the Nobori-cho section—Father Superior LaSalle and Father Schiffer—had happily escaped this affliction.

Father Kleinsorge woke up about six the morning the bomb was dropped, and half-an-hour later—he was a bit tardy because of his sickness—he began to read Mass in the mission chapel, a small Japanese-style wooden building which was without pews, since its worshippers knelt on the usual Japanese matted floor, facing an altar graced with splendid silks, brass, silver, and heavy embroideries. This morning, a Monday, the only worshippers were Mr. Takemoto, a theological student living in the mission house; Mr. Fukai, the secretary of the diocese; Mrs. Murata, the mission's

devoutly Christian housekeeper; and his fellow-priests.
After Mass, while Father Kleinsorge was reading the
Prayers of Thanksgiving, the siren sounded. He stopped
the service and the missionaries retired across the
compound to the bigger building. There, in his room
on the ground floor, to the right of the front door,
Father Kleinsorge changed into a military uniform
which he had acquired when he was teaching at the
Rokko Middle School in Kobe and which he wore
during air-raid alerts.

After an alarm, Father Kleinsorge always went out
and scanned the sky, and this time, when he stepped
outside, he was glad to see only the single weather
plane that flew over Hiroshima each day about this
time. Satisfied that nothing would happen, he went in
and breakfasted with the other Fathers on substitute
coffee and ration bread, which, under the circumstances,
was especially repugnant to him. The Fathers sat and
talked a while, until, at eight, they heard the all-clear.
They went then to various parts of the building.
Father Schiffer retired to his room to do some writing.
Father Cieslik sat in his room in a straight chair with
a pillow over his stomach to ease his pain, and read.
Father Superior LaSalle stood at the window of his
room, thinking. Father Kleinsorge went up to a room
on the third floor, took off all his clothes except his
underwear, and stretched out on his right side on a
cot and began reading his *Stimmen der Zeit*.

After the terrible flash—which, Father Kleinsorge
later realized, reminded him of something he had read
as a boy about a large meteor colliding with the earth
—he had time (since he was 1,400 yards from the

centre) for one thought: A bomb has fallen directly on us. Then, for a few seconds or minutes, he went out of his mind.

Father Kleinsorge never knew how he got out of the house. The next things he was conscious of were that he was wandering around in the mission's vegetable garden in his underwear, bleeding slightly from small cuts along his left flank; that all the buildings round about had fallen down except the Jesuits' mission house, which had long before been braced and double-braced by a priest named Gropper, who was terrified of earthquakes; that the day had turned dark; and that Murata-*san*, the housekeeper, was near by, crying over and over, " *Shu Jesusu, awaremi tamai !* Our Lord Jesus, have pity on us !"

On the train on the way into Hiroshima from the country, where he lived with his mother, Dr. Terufumi Sasaki, the Red Cross Hospital surgeon, thought over an unpleasant nightmare he had had the night before. His mother's home was in Mukaihara, thirty miles from the city, and it took him two hours by train and tram to reach the hospital. He had slept uneasily all night and had wakened an hour earlier than usual, and, feeling sluggish and slightly feverish, had debated whether to go to the hospital at all ; his sense of duty finally forced him to go, and he had started out on an earlier train than he took most mornings. The dream had particularly frightened him because it was so closely associated, on the surface at least, with a disturbing actuality. He was only twenty-five years old and had just completed his training at the Eastern Medical University, in Tsingtao, China. He was some-

thing of an idealist and was much distressed by the
inadequacy of medical facilities in the country town
where his mother lived. Quite on his own, and without
a permit, he had begun visiting a few sick people out
there in the evenings, after his eight hours at the
hospital and four hours' commuting. He had recently
learned that the penalty for practising without a
permit was severe; a fellow-doctor whom he had asked
about it had given him a serious scolding. Nevertheless,
he had continued to practise. In his dream, he had
been at the bedside of a country patient when the
police and the doctor he had consulted burst into the
room, seized him, dragged him outside, and beat him
up cruelly. On the train, he just about decided to give
up the work in Mukáihara, since he felt it would be
impossible to get a permit, because the authorities
would hold that it would conflict with his duties at
the Red Cross Hospital.

At the terminus, he caught a street-car at once. (He
later calculated that if he had taken his customary
train that morning, and if he had had to wait a few
minutes for the street-car, as often happened, he would
have been close to the centre at the time of the explosion
and would surely have perished.) He arrived at the
hospital at seven-forty and reported to the chief
surgeon. A few minutes later, he went to a room on
the first floor and drew blood from the arm of a man
in order to perform a Wassermann test. The laboratory
containing the incubators for the test was on the third
floor. With the blood specimen in his left hand,
walking in a kind of distraction he had felt all morning,
probably because of the dream and his restless night,

he started along the main corridor on his way toward the stairs. He was one step beyond an open window when the light of the bomb was reflected, like a gigantic photographic flash, in the corridor. He ducked down on one knee and said to himself, as only a Japanese would, " Sasaki, *gambare !* Be brave !" Just then (the building was 1,650 yards from the centre), the blast ripped through the hospital. The glasses he was wearing flew off his face; the bottle of blood crashed against one wall; his Japanese slippers zipped out from under his feet—but otherwise, thanks to where he stood, he was untouched.

Dr. Sasaki shouted the name of the chief surgeon and rushed around to the man's office and found him terribly cut by glass. The hospital was in horrible confusion: heavy partitions and ceilings had fallen on patients, beds had overturned, windows had blown in and cut people, blood was spattered on the walls and floors, instruments were everywhere, many of the patients were running about screaming, many more lay dead. (A colleague working in the laboratory to which Dr. Sasaki had been walking was dead; Dr. Sasaki's patient, whom he had just left and who a few moments before had been dreadfully afraid of syphilis, was also dead.) Dr. Sasaki found himself the only doctor in the hospital who was unhurt.

Dr. Sasaki, who believed that the enemy had hit only the building he was in, got bandages and began to bind the wounds of those inside the hospital; while outside, all over Hiroshima, maimed and dying citizens turned their unsteady steps toward the Red Cross Hospital to begin an invasion that was to make

Dr. Sasaki forget his private nightmare for a long, long time.

Miss Toshiko Sasaki, the East Asia Tin Works clerk, who is not related to Dr. Sasaki, got up at three o'clock in the morning on the day the bomb fell. There was extra housework to do. Her eleven-month-old brother, Akio, had come down the day before with a serious stomach upset; her mother had taken him to the Tamura Pediatric Hospital and was staying there with him. Miss Sasaki, who was about twenty, had to cook breakfast for her father, a brother, a sister, and herself, and—since the hospital, because of the war, was unable to provide food—to prepare a whole day's meals for her mother and the baby, in time for her father, who worked in a factory making rubber earplugs for artillery crews, to take the food by on his way to the plant. When she had finished and had cleaned and put away the cooking things, it was nearly seven. The family lived in Koi, and she had a forty-five-minute trip to the tin works, in the section of town called Kannon-machi. She was in charge of the personnel records in the factory. She left Koi at seven, and as soon as she reached the plant, she went with some of the other girls from the personnel department to the factory auditorium. A prominent local Navy man, a former employee, had committed suicide the day before by throwing himself under a train—a death considered honourable enough to warrant a memorial service, which was to be held at the tin works at ten o'clock that morning. In the large hall, Miss Sasaki and the others made suitable preparations for the meeting. This work took about twenty minutes.

Miss Sasaki went back to her office and sat down at her desk. She was quite far from the windows, which were off to her left, and behind her were a couple of tall bookcases containing all the books of the factory library, which the personnel department had organized. She settled herself at her desk, put some things in a drawer, and shifted papers. She thought that before she began to make entries in her lists of new employees, discharges, and departures for the Army, she would chat for a moment with the girl at her right. Just as she turned her head away from the windows, the room was filled with a blinding light. She was paralyzed by fear, fixed still in her chair for a long moment (the plant was 1,600 yards from the centre).

Everything fell, and Miss Sasaki lost consciousness. The ceiling dropped suddenly and the wooden floor above collapsed in splinters and the people up there came down and the roof above them gave way; but principally and first of all, the bookcases right behind her swooped forward and the contents threw her down, with her left leg horribly twisted and breaking underneath her. There, in the tin factory, in the first moment under atomic age, a human being was crushed by books.

II

THE FIRE

IMMEDIATELY after the explosion, the Reverend Mr. Kiyoshi Tanimoto, having run wildly out of the Matsui estate and having looked in wonderment at the bloody soldiers at the mouth of the dugout they had been digging, attached himself sympathetically to an old lady who was walking along in a daze, holding her head with her left hand, supporting a small boy of three or four on her back with her right, and crying, "I'm hurt! I'm hurt! I'm hurt!" Mr. Tanimoto transferred the child to his own back and led the woman by the hand down the street, which was darkened by what seemed to be a local column of dust. He took the woman to a grammar school not far away that had previously been designated for use as a temporary hospital in² case of emergency. By this solicitous behaviour, Mr. Tanimoto at once got rid of his terror. At the school, he was much surprised to see glass all over the floor and fifty or sixty injured people already waiting to be treated. He reflected that, although the all-clear had sounded and he had heard no planes, several bombs must have been dropped. He thought of a hillock in the rayon man's garden from which he could get a view of the whole of Koi— of the whole of Hiroshima, for that matter—and he ran back up to the estate.

From the mound, Mr. Tanimoto saw an astonishing panorama. Not just a patch of Koi, as he had expected, but as much of Hiroshima as he could see through the clouded air was giving off a thick, dreadful miasma.

Clumps of smoke, near and far, had begun to push
up through the general dust. He wondered how such
extensive damage could have been dealt out of a silent
sky; even a few planes, far³ up, would have been
audible. Houses nearby were burning, and when huge
drops of water the size of marbles began to fall, he
half thought that they must be coming from the hoses
of firemen fighting the blazes. (They were actually
drops of condensed moisture falling from the turbulent
tower of dust, heat, and fission fragments, that had
already risen miles into the sky above Hiroshima.)

Mr. Tanimoto turned away from the sight when he
heard Mr. Matsuo call out to ask whether he was all
right. Mr. Matsuo had been safely cushioned within
the falling house by the bedding stored in the front hall
and had worked his way out. Mr. Tanimoto scarcely
answered. He had thought of his wife and baby, his
church, his home, his parishioners, all of them down
in that awful murk. Once more he began to run in
fear—toward the city.

Mrs. Hatsuyo Nakamura, the tailor's widow, having
struggled up from under the ruins of her house after
the explosion, and seeing Myeko, the youngest of her
three children, buried breast-deep and unable to move,
crawled across the debris, hauled at timbers, and flung
tiles aside, in a hurried effort to free the child. Then,
from what seemed to be caverns far below, she heard
two small voices crying. " *Tasukete !   Tasukete !*
Help !   Help !"

She called the names of her ten-year-old son and
eight-year-old daughter: " Toshio !   Yaeko !"

The voices from below answered.

Mrs. Nakamura abandoned Myeko, who at least could breathe, and in a frenzy made the wreckage fly above the crying voices. The children had been sleeping nearly ten feet apart, but now their voices seemed to come from the same place. Toshio, the boy, apparently had some freedom to move, because she could feel him undermining the pile of wood and tiles as she worked from above. At last she saw his head, and she hastily pulled him out by it. A mosquito net was wound intricately, as if it had been carefully wrapped, around his feet. He said he had been blown right across the room and had been on top of his sister. Yaeko under the wreckage. She now said, from underneath, that she could not move, because there was something on her legs. With a bit more digging, Mrs. Nakamura cleared a hole above the child and began to pull her arm. "*Itai !* It hurts !" Yaeko cried. Mrs. Nakamura shouted, " There's no time now to say whether it hurts or not," and yanked her whimpering daughter up. Then she freed Myeko. The children were filthy and bruised, but none of them had a single cut or scratch.

Mrs. Nakamura took the children out into the street. They had nothing on but underpants, and although the day was very hot, she worried rather confusedly about their being cold, so she went back into the wreckage and burrowed underneath and found a bundle of clothes she had packed for an emergency, and she dressed them in pants, blouses, shoes, padded-cotton air-raid helmets called *bokuzuki*, and even, irrationally, overcoats. The children were silent, except for the five-year-old, Myeko, who kept asking questions :

" Why is it night already ? Why did our house fall
down ? What happened ?" Mrs. Nakamura, who did
not know what had happened (had not the all-clear
sounded ?), looked around and saw through the darkness that all the houses in her neighbourhood had
collapsed. The house next door, which its owner had
been tearing down to make way for a fire lane, was now
very thoroughly, if crudely, torn down; its owner,
who had been sacrificing his home for the community's
safety, lay dead. Mrs. Nakamoto, wife of the head of
the local air-raid defence Neighbourhood Association,
came across the street with her head all bloody, and
said that her baby was badly cut; did Mrs. Nakamura
have any bandage ? Mrs. Nakamura did not, but she
crawled into the remains of her house again and pulled
out some white cloth that she had been using in her
work as a seamstress, ripped it into strips, and gave
it to Mrs. Nakamoto. While fetching the cloth, she
noticed her sewing machine; she went back in for it
and dragged it out. Obviously, she could not carry
it with her, so she unthinkingly plunged her symbol
of livelihood into the receptacle which for weeks had
been her symbol of safety—the cement tank of water
in front of her house, of the type every household had
been ordered to construct against a possible fire raid.

A nervous neighbour, Mrs. Hataya, called to Mrs.
Nakamura to run away with her to the woods in Asano
Park—an estate by the Kyo River not far off, belonging
to the wealthy Asano family, who once owned the
Toyo Kisen Kaisha steamship line. The park had been
designated as an evacuation area for their neighbourhood. Seeing fire breaking out in a nearby ruin (except

at the very centre, where the bomb itself ignited some fires, most of Hiroshima's citywide conflagration was caused by inflammable wreckage falling on cook-stoves and live wires), Mrs. Nakamura suggested going over to fight it. Mrs. Hataya said, " Don't be foolish. What if planes come and drop more bombs?" So Mrs. Nakamura started out for Asano Park with her children and Mrs. Hataya, and she carried her ruck-sack of emergency clothing, a blanket, an umbrella, and a suitcase of things she had cached in her air-raid shelter. Under many ruins, as they hurried along, they heard muffled screams for help. The only building they saw standing on their way to Asano Park was the Jesuit mission house, alongside the Catholic kinder-garten to which Mrs. Nakamura had sent Myeko for a time. As they passed it, she saw Father Kleinsorge, in bloody underwear, running out of the house with a small suitcase in his hand.

Right after the explosion, while Father Wilhelm Kleinsorge, S. J., was wandering around in his under-wear in the vegetable garden, Father Superior LaSalle came around the corner of the building in the darkness. His body, especially his back, was bloody; the flash had made him twist away from his window, and tiny pieces of glass had flown at him. Father Kleinsorge, still bewildered, managed to ask, " Where are the rest ?" Just then, the two other priests living in the mission house appeared—Father Cieslik, unhurt, supporting Father Schiffer, who was covered with blood that spurted from a cut above his left ear and who was very pale. Father Cieslik was rather pleased with himself, for after the flash he had dived into a doorway, which he had previously reckoned to be the safest place inside the building, and when the blast came, he was not injured. Father LaSalle told Father Cieslik to take Father Schiffer to a doctor before he bled to death, and suggested either Dr. Kanda, who lived on the next corner, or Dr. Fujii, about six blocks away. The two men went out of the compound and up the street.

The daughter of Mr. Hoshijima, the mission catechist, ran up to Father Kleinsorge and said that her mother and sister were buried under the ruins of their house, which was at the back of the Jesuit compound, and at the same time the priests noticed that the house of the Catholic-kindergarten teacher at the foot of the compound had collapsed on her. While Father LaSalle and Mrs. Murata, the mission housekeeper, dug the teacher out, Father Kleinsorge went to the catechist's fallen house and began lifting things off the top of the pile. There was not a sound underneath; he was sure the Hoshijima women had been killed. At last, under what had been a corner of the kitchen, he saw Mrs. Hoshijima's head. Believing her dead, he began to haul her out by the hair, but suddenly she screamed, " *Itai ! Itai !* It hurts ! It hurts !" He dug some more and lifted her out. He managed, too, to find her daughter 'in the rubble and free her. Neither was badly hurt.

A public bath next door to the mission house had caught fire, but since there the wind was southerly, the priests thought their house would be spared. Nevertheless, as a precaution, Father Kleinsorge went inside to fetch some things he wanted to save. He found his room in a state of weird and illogical confusion. A first-aid kit was hanging undisturbed on a hook on the wall, but his clothes, which had been on other hooks nearby, were nowhere to be seen. His desk was in splinters all over the room, but a mere papier-mache suitcase, which he had hidden under the desk, stood handle-side up, without a scratch on it, in the doorway of the room, where he could not miss it. Father Kleinsorge later came to regard this as a bit of Providential interference, inasmuch as the suitcase contained his breviary, the account books for the whole diocese, and a considerable amount of paper money belonging to the mission, for which he was responsible. He ran out of the house and deposited the suitcase in the mission air-raid shelter.

At about this time, Father Cieslik and Father Schiffer, who was still spurting blood, came back and said that Dr. Kanda's house was ruined and that fire blocked them from getting out of what they supposed to be the local circle of destruction to Dr. Fujii's private hospital, on the bank of the Kyo River.

Dr. Masakazu Fujii's hospital was no longer on the bank of the Kyo River; it was in the river. After the overturn, Dr. Fujii was so stupefied and so tightly squeezed by the beams gripping his chest that he was unable to move at first, and he hung there about twenty minutes in the darkened morning. Then a thought which came to him—that soon the tide would be running in through the estuaries and his head would be submerged—inspired him to fearful activity; he wriggled and turned and exerted what strength he could (though his left arm, because of the pain in his shoulder, was useless), and before long he had freed himself from the vice... After a few moments' rest, he climbed on to the pile of timbers and, finding a long one that slanted up to the river bank, he painfully shinnied up it. ᵉ

Dr. Fujii, who was in his underwear, was now soaking and dirty. His undershirt was torn, and blood ran down it from bad cuts on his chin and back. In this disarray, he walked out onto Kyo Bridge, beside which his hospital had stood. The bridge had not collapsed. He could see only fuzzily without his glasses, but he could see enough to be amazed at the number of houses that were down all around. On the bridge, he encountered a friend, a doctor named Machii, and asked in bewilderment, "What do you think it was?"

Dr. Machii said, "It must have been a *Molotoffano hanakago*"—a Molotov flower basket, the delicate Japanese name for the "bread basket," or self-scattering cluster of bombs.

At first, Dr. Fujii could see only two fires, one across the river from his hospital site and one quite far to the south. 'But at the same time, he and his friend observed something that puzzled them, and which, as doctors, they discussed: although there were as yet very few fires, wounded people were hurrying across the bridge in an endless parade of misery, and many of them exhibited terrible burns on their faces and arms. "Why do you suppose it is?" Dr. Fujii asked. Even a theory was comforting that day, and Dr. Machii stuck to his. "Perhaps because it was a Molotov flower basket," after he said.

There had been no breeze earlier in the morning

when Dr. Fujii had walked to the railway station to see a friend off, but now brisk winds were blowing every which way; here on the bridge the wind was easterly. New fires were leaping up, and they spread quickly, and in a very short time terrible blasts of hot air and showers of cinders made it impossible to stand on the bridge any more. Dr. Machii ran to the far side of the river and along a still unkindled street. Dr. Fujii went down into the water under the bridge, where a score of people had already taken refuge, among them his servants, who had extricated themselves from the wreckage. From there, Dr. Fujii saw a nurse hanging in the timbers of his hospital by her legs, and then another painfully pinned across the breast. He enlisted the help of some of the others under the bridge and freed both of them. He thought he heard the voice of his niece for a moment, but he could not find her; he never saw her again. Four of his nurses and the two patients in the hospital died, too. Dr. Fujii went back into the water of the river and waited for the fire to subside.

The lot of Drs. Fujii, Kanda, and Machii right after the explosion—and, as these three were typical, that of the majority of the physicians and surgeons of Hiroshima—with their offices and hospitals destroyed, their equipment scattered, their own bodies incapacitated in varying degrees, explained why so many citizens who were hurt went untended and why so many who might have lived died. Of a hundred and fifty doctors in the city, sixty-five were already dead and most of the rest were wounded. Of 1,780 nurses, 1,654 were dead or too badly hurt to work. In the biggest hospital, that of the Red Cross, only six doctors out of thirty were able to function, and only ten nurses out of more than two hundred. The sole uninjured doctor on the Red Cross Hospital staff was Dr. Sasaki. After the explosion, he hurried to a storeroom to fetch bandages. This room, like everything he had seen as he ran through the hospital, was chaotic—bottles of medicines thrown off shelves and broken, salves spattered on the walls, instruments strewn everywhere. He grabbed up some bandages and an unbroken bottle of mercurochrome, hurried back to the chief surgeon, and bandaged his cuts. Then he went out into the corridor and began patching up the wounded patients and the doctors and nurses there. He blundered so without his glasses that he took a pair off the face of a wounded nurse, and although they only approximately compensated for the errors of his vision, they were better than nothing. (He was to depend on them for more than a month.)

Dr. Sasaki worked without method, taking those who were nearest him first, and he noticed soon that the corridor seemed to be getting more and more crowded. Mixed in with the abrasions and lacerations which most people in the hospital had suffered, he began to find dreadful burns. He realized then that casualties were pouring in from outdoors. There were so many that he began to pass up the lightly wounded; he decided that all he could hope to do was to stop people from bleeding to death. Before long, patients lay and crouched on the floors of the wards and the laboratories and all the other rooms, and in the corridors, and on the stairs, and in the front hall, and under the porte-cochère, and on the stone front steps, and in the driveway and courtyard, and for blocks each way in the streets outside. Wounded people supported maimed people; disfigured families leaned together. Many people were vomiting. A tremendous number of schoolgirls—some of those who had been taken from their classrooms to work outdoors, clearing fire lanes—crept into the hospital. In a city of two hundred and forty-five thousand, nearly a hundred thousand people had been killed or doomed at one blow; a hundred thousand more were hurt. At least ten thousand of the wounded made their way to the best hospital in town, which was altogether unequal to such a trampling, since it had only six hundred beds, and they had all been occupied. The people in the suffocating crowd inside the hospital wept and cried, for Dr. Sasaki to hear, " *Sensei !* Doctor !" and the less seriously wounded came and pulled at his sleeve and begged him to come to the aid of the worse wounded. Tugged here and there in his stockinged feet, bewildered by the numbers, staggered by so much raw flesh, Dr. Sasaki lost all sense of profession and stopped working as a skilful surgeon and a sympathetic man; he became an automaton, mechanically wiping, daubing, winding, wiping, daubing, winding.

Some of the wounded in Hiroshima were unable to enjoy the questionable luxury of hospitalisation. In what had been the personnel office of the East Asia Tin Works, Miss Sasaki lay doubled over, unconscious, under the tremendous pile of books and plaster and wood and corrugated iron. She was wholly unconscious (she later estimated) for about three hours. Her first sensation was of dreadful pain in her left leg. It was so black under the books and debris that the borderline between awareness and unconsciousness was fine; she apparently crossed it several times, for the pain seemed to come and go. At the moments when it was sharpest, she felt that her leg had been cut off somewhere below the knee. Later, she heard someone walking on top of the wreckage above her, and anguished voices spoke up, evidently from within the mess around her: "Please help! Get us out!"

Father Kleinsorge stemmed Father Schiffer's spurting cut as well as he could with some bandage that Dr. Fujii had given the priests a few days before. When he finished, he ran into the mission house again and found the jacket of his military uniform and an old pair of grey trousers. He put them on and went outside. A woman from next door ran up to him and shouted that her husband was buried under her house and the house was on fire; Father Kleinsorge must come and save him.

Father Kleinsorge, already growing apathetic and dazed in the presence of the cumulative distress, said, " We haven't much time." Houses all around were burning, and the wind was now blowing hard. " Do you know exactly which part of the house he is under ?" he asked.

" Yes, yes," she said. " Come quickly."

They went around to the house, the remains of which blazed violently, but when they got there, it turned out that the woman had no idea where her husband was. Father Kleinsorge shouted several times, " Is anyone there ?" There was no answer.

Father Kleinsorge said to the woman, " We must get away or we will all die." He went back to the Catholic compound and told the Father Superior that the fire was coming closer on the wind, which had swung around and was now from the north; it was time for everybody to go.

Just then, the kindergarten teacher pointed out to the priests Mr. Fukai, the secretary of the diocese, who was standing in his window on the second floor of the mission house, facing in the direction of the explosion, weeping. Father Cieslik, because he thought the stairs unusable, ran around to the back of the mission house to look for a ladder. There he heard people crying for help under a nearby fallen roof. He called to passers-by running away in the street to help him lift it, but nobody paid any attention, and he had to leave the buried ones to die. Father Kleinsorge ran inside the mission house and scrambled up the stairs, which were awry and piled with plaster and lathing, and called to Mr. Fukai from the doorway of his room.

Mr. Fukai, a very short man of about fifty, turned around slowly, with a queer look, and said, " Leave me here."

Father Kleinsorge went into the room and took Mr. Fukai by the collar of his coat and said, " Come with me or you'll die."

Mr. Fukai said, " Leave me here to die."

Father Kleinsorge began to shove and haul Mr. Fukai out of the room. Then the theological student came up and grabbed Mr. Fukai's feet, and Father Kleinsorge took his shoulders, and together they carried him downstairs and outdoors. " I can't walk !"

Mr. Fukai cried. " Leave me here !" Father Kleinsorge got his paper suitcase with the money in it and took Mr. Fukai up pick-a-back, and the party started for the East Parade Ground, their district's " safe area." As they went out of the gate, Mr. Fukai, quite child-like now, beat on Father Kleinsorge's shoulders and said, " I won't leave. I won't leave." Irrelevantly, Father Kleinsorge turned to Father LaSalle and said, " We have lost all our possessions but not our sense of humour."

The street was cluttered with parts of houses that had slid into it, and with fallen telephone poles and wires. From every second or third house came the voices of people buried and abandoned, who invariably screamed, with formal politeness, " *Tasukete kure !* Help, if you please !" The priests recognised several ruins from which these cries came as the homes of friends, but because of the fire it was too late to help. All the way, Mr. Fukai whimpered, " Let me stay." The party turned right when they came to a block of fallen houses that was one flame. At Sakai Bridge, which would take them across to the East Parade Ground, they saw that the whole community on the opposite side of the river was a sheet of fire; they dared not cross and decided to take refuge in Asano Park, off to their left. Father Kleinsorge, who had been weakened for a couple of days by his bad case of diarrhoea, began to stagger under his protesting burden, and as he tried to climb up over the wreckage of several houses that blocked their way to the park, he stumbled, dropped Mr. Fukai, and plunged down, head over heels, to the edge of the river. When he picked himself up, he saw Mr. Fukai running away. Father Kleinsorge shouted to a dozen soldiers, who were standing by the bridge, to stop him. As Father Kleinsorge started back to get Mr. Fukai, Father LaSalle called out, " Hurry ! Don't waste time !" So Father Kleinsorge just requested the soldiers to take care of Mr. Fukai. They said they would, but the little, broken man got away from them, and the last the priests could see of him, he was running back toward the fire.

Mr. Tanimoto, fearful for his family and church, at first ran toward them by the shortest route, along Koi Highway. He was the only person making his way into the city; he met hundreds and hundreds who were fleeing, and every one of them seemed to be hurt in some way. The eyebrows of some were burned off and skin hung from their faces and hands. Others, because of pain, held their arms up as if carrying something in both hands. Some were vomiting as they walked. Many were naked or in shreds of clothing. On some undressed bodies, the burns had made patterns—of undershirt straps and suspenders and, on the skin of some women (since white repelled the heat from the bomb and dark clothes absorbed it and conducted it to the skin), the shapes of flowers they had had on their kimonos. Many, although injured themselves, supported relatives who were worse off. Almost all had their heads bowed, looked straight ahead, were silent, and showed no expression whatever.

After crossing Koi Bridge and Kannon Bridge, having run the whole way, Mr. Tanimoto saw, as he

approached the centre, that all the houses had been
crushed and many were afire. Here the trees were
bare and their trunks were charred. He tried at several
points to penetrate the ruins, but the flames always
stopped him. Under many houses, people screamed
for help, but no one helped; in general, survivors that
day assisted only their relatives or immediate neighbours, for they could not comprehend or tolerate a
wider circle of misery. The wounded limped past the
screams, and Mr. Tanimoto ran past them. As a
Christian he was filled with compassion for those who
were trapped, and as a Japanese he was overwhelmed
by the shame of being unhurt, and he prayed as he
ran, "God help them and take them out of the fire."

He thought he would skirt the fire, to the left. He
ran back to Kannon Bridge and followed for a distance
one of the rivers. He tried several cross streets, but all
were blocked, so he turned far left and ran out to
Yokogawa, a station on a railroad line that detoured
the city in a wide semi-circle, and he followed the rails
until he came to a burning train. So impressed was he
by this time by the extent of the damage that he ran
north two miles to Gion, a suburb in the foothills.
All the way, he overtook dreadfully burned and
lacerated people, and in his guilt he turned to right
and left as he hurried and said to some of them,
"Excuse me for having no burden like yours." Near
Gion, he began to meet country people going toward
the city to help, and when they saw him, several
exclaimed, "Look ! There is one who is not wounded."
At Gion, he bore toward the right bank of the main
river, the Ota, and ran down it until he reached fire

again. There was no fire on the other side of the river, so he threw off his shirt and shoes and plunged into it. In midstream, where the current was fairly strong, exhaustion and fear finally caught up with him—he had run nearly seven miles—and he became limp and drifted in the water. He prayed, " Please, God, help me to cross. It would be nonsense for me to be drowned when I am the only uninjured one." He managed a few more strokes and fetched up on a spit downstream.

Mr. Tanimoto climbed up the bank and ran along it until, near a large Shinto shrine, he came to more fire, and as he turned left to get around it, he met, by incredible luck, his wife. She was carrying their infant son. Mr. Tanimoto was now so emotionally worn out that nothing could surprise him. He did not embrace his wife; he simply said, " Oh, you are safe." She told him that she had got home from her night in Ushida just in time for the explosion; she had been buried under the parsonage with the baby in her arms. She told how the wreckage had pressed down on her, how the baby had cried. She saw a chink of light, and by reaching up with a hand, she worked the hole bigger, bit by bit. After about half-an-hour, she heard the crackling noise of wood burning. At last the opening was big enough for her to push the baby out, and afterward she crawled out herself. She said she was now going out to Ushida again. Mr. Tanimoto said he wanted to see his church and take care of the people of his Neighbourhood Association. They parted as casually—as bewildered—as they had met.

Mr. Tanimoto's way around the fire took him across the East Parade Ground, which, being an evacuation area, was now the scene of a gruesome review: rank on rank of the burned and bleeding. Those who were burned moaned, " *Mizu, mizu !* Water, water !" Mr. Tanimoto found a basin in a near-by street and located a water tap that still worked in the crushed shell of a house, and he began carrying water to the suffering strangers. When he had given drink to about thirty of them, he realised he was taking too much time. " Excuse me," he said loudly to those near by who were reaching out their hands to him and crying their thirst. " I have many people to take care of." Then he ran away. He went to the river again, the basin in his hand, and jumped down on to a sandspit. There he saw hundreds of people so badly wounded that they could not get up to go farther from the burning city. When they saw a man erect and unhurt, the chant began again: " *Mizu, mizu, mizu.*" Mr. Tanimoto could not resist them; he carried them water from the river—a mistake, since it was tidal and brackish. Two or three small boats were ferrying hurt people across the river from Asano Park, and when one touched the spit, Mr. Tanimoto again made his loud, apologetic speech and jumped into the boat. It took him across to the park. There, in the underbrush, he found some of his charges of the Neighbourhood Association, who had come there by his previous instructions, and saw many acquaintances, among them Father Kleinsorge and the other Catholics. But he missed Fukai, who had been a close friend. " Where is Fukai-*san* ?" he asked.

" He didn't want to come with us," Father Kleinsorge said. " He ran back."

When Miss Sasaki heard the voices of the people caught along with her in the dilapidation at the tin factory, she began speaking to them. Her nearest neighbour, she discovered, was a high-school girl who had been drafted for factory work, and who said her back was broken. Miss Sasaki replied, "I am lying here and I can't move. My left leg is cut off."

Some time later, she again heard somebody walk overhead and then move off to one side, and whoever it was began burrowing. The digger released several people, and when he had uncovered the high-school girl, she found that her back was not broken, after all, and she crawled out. Miss Sasaki spoke to the rescuer, and he worked toward her. He pulled away a great number of books, until he had made a tunnel to her. She could see his perspiring face as he said, " Come out, Miss." She tried. " I can't move," she said. The man excavated some more and told her to try with all her strength to get out. But books were heavy on her hips, and the man finally saw that a bookcase was leaning on the books and that a heavy beam pressed down on the bookcase. " Wait," he said. " I'll get a crowbar."

The man was gone a long time, and when he came back, he was ill-tempered, as if her plight were all her fault. " We have no men to help you, " he shouted in through the tunnel. " You'll have to get out by yourself."

" That's impossible," she said. " My left leg . . ." The man went away.

Much later, several men came and dragged Miss Sasaki out. Her left leg was not severed, but it was badly broken and cut and it hung askew below the knee. They took her out into a courtyard. It was raining. She sat on the ground in the rain. When the downpour increased, someone directed all the wounded people to take cover in the factory's air-raid shelters. " Come along," a torn-up woman said to her. " You can hop." But Miss Sasaki could not move, and she just waited in the rain. Then a man propped up a large sheet of corrugated iron as a kind of lean-to, and took her in his arms and carried her to it. She was grateful until he brought two horribly wounded people—a woman with a whole breast sheared off and a man whose face was all raw from a burn—to share the simple shed with her. No one came back. The rain cleared and the cloudy afternoon was hot; before nightfall the three grotesques under the slanting piece of twisted iron began to smell quite bad.

The former head of the Nobori-cho Neighbourhood Association, to which the Catholic priests belonged, was an energetic man named Yoshida. He had boasted, when he was in charge of the district air-raid defences, that fire might eat away all of Hiroshima but it would never come to Nobori-cho. The bomb blew down his house, and a joist pinned him by the legs, in full view of the Jesuit mission house across the way and of the people hurrying along the street. In their confusion as they hurried past, Mrs. Nakamura, with her children, and Father Kleinsorge, with Mr. Fukai on his back, hardly saw him; he was just part of the general blur of misery through which they moved. His cries for help brought no response from them; there were so many people shouting for help that they could not hear

him separately. They and all the others went along.
Nobori-cho became absolutely deserted, and the fire
swept through it.   Mr. Yoshida saw the wooden
mission house—the only erect building in the area—
go up in a lick of flame, and the heat was terrific on
his face. Then flames came along his side of the street
and entered his house. In a paroxysm of terrified
strength, he freed himself and ran down the alleys of
Nobori-cho, hemmed in by the fire he had said would
never come. He began at once to behave like an old
man; two months later his hair was white.

As Dr. Fujii stood in the river up to his neck to
avoid the heat of the fire, the wind grew stronger and
stronger, and soon, even though the expanse of water
was small, the waves grew so high that the people
under the bridge could no longer keep their footing.
Dr. Fujii went close to the shore, crouched down, and
embraced a large stone with his usable arm. Later it
became possible to wade along the very edge of the
river, and Dr. Fujii and his two surviving nurses
moved about two hundred yards upstream, to a sandspit near Asano Park. Many wounded were lying on
the sand. Dr. Machii was there with his family; his
daughter, who had been outdoors when the bomb
burst, was badly burned on her hands and legs but
fortunately not on her face. Although Dr. Fujii's
shoulder was by now terribly painful, he examined the
girl's burns curiously. Then he lay down. In spite of
the misery all around, he was ashamed of his appear-
ance, and he remarked to Dr. Machii that he looked
like a beggar, dressed as he was in nothing but torn
and bloody underwear. Late in the afternoon, when

the fire began to subside, he decided to go to his parental house, in the suburb of Nagatsuka. He asked Dr. Machii to join him, but the Doctor answered that he and his family were going to spend the night on the spit, because of his daughter's injuries. Dr. Fujii, together with his nurses, walked first to Ushida, where, in the partially damaged house of some relatives, he found first-aid materials he had stored there. The two nurses bandaged him and he them. They went on. Now not many people walked in the streets, but a great number sat and lay on the pavement, vomited, waited for death, and died. The number of corpses on the way to Nagatsuka was more and more puzzling. The Doctor wondered: Could a Molotov flower basket have done all this?

Dr. Fujii reached his family's house in the evening. It was five miles from the centre of town, but its roof had fallen in and the windows were all broken.

All day, people poured into Asano Park. This private estate was far enough away from the explosion so that its bamboos, pines, laurel, and maples were still alive, and the green place invited refugees—partly because they believed that if the Americans came back, they would bomb only buildings; partly because the foliage seemed a centre of coolness and life, and the estate's exquisitely precise rock gardens, with their quiet pools and arching bridges, were very Japanese, normal, secure; and also partly (according to some who were there) because of an irresistible, atavistic urge to hide under leaves. Mrs. Nakamura and her children were among the first to arrive, and they settled in the bamboo grove near the river. They all felt terribly thirsty, and they drank from the river. At once they were nauseated and began vomiting, and they retched the whole day. Others were also nauseated; they all thought (probably because of the strong odour of ionization, an " electric smell " given off by the bomb's fission) that they were sick from a gas the Americans had dropped. When Father Kleinsorge and the other priests came into the park, nodding to their friends as they passed, the Nakamuras were all sick and prostrate. A woman named Iwasaki, who lived in the neighbourhood of the mission and who was sitting near the Nakamuras, got up and asked the priests if she should stay where she was or go with them. Father Kleinsorge said, " I hardly know where the safest place is." She stayed there, and later in the day, though she had no visible wounds or burns, she died. The priests went farther along the river and settled down in some underbrush. Father LaSalle lay down and went right to sleep. The theological student, who was wearing slippers, had carried with him a bundle of clothes, in which he had packed two pairs of leather shoes. When he sat down with the others, he found that the bundle had broken open and a couple of shoes had fallen out and now he had only two lefts. He retraced his steps and found one right. When he rejoined the priests, he said, " It's funny, but things don't matter any more. Yesterday, my shoes were my most important possessions. To-day, I don't care. One pair is enough."

Father Cieslik said, " I know. I started to bring my books along, and then I thought, ' This is no time for books.' "

When Mr. Tanimoto, with his basin still in his hand, reached the park, it was very crowded, and to distinguish the living from the dead was not easy, for most of the people lay still, with their eyes open. To Father Kleinsorge, an Occidental, the silence in the grove by the river, where hundreds of gruesomely wounded suffered together, was one of the most dreadful and awesome phenomena of his whole experience. The hurt ones were quiet; no one wept, much less screamed in pain; no one complained; none of the many who died did so noisily; not even the children cried; very few people even spoke. And when Father Kleinsorge gave water to some whose faces had been almost blotted out by flash burns, they took their share and then raised themselves a little and bowed to him, in thanks.

Mr. Tanimoto greeted the priests and then looked around for other friends. He saw Mrs. Matsumoto, wife of the director of the Methodist School, and asked her if she was thirsty. She was, so he went to one of the pools in the Asanos' rock gardens and got water for her in his basin. Then he decided to try to get back to his church. He went into Nobori-cho by the way the priests had taken as they escaped, but he did not get far; the fire along the streets was so fierce that he had to turn back. He walked to the river bank and began to look for a boat in which he might carry some of the most severely injured across the river from Asano Park and away from the spreading fire. Soon he found a good-sized pleasure punt drawn up on the bank, but in and around it was an awful tableau—five dead men, nearly naked, badly burned, who must have expired more or less all at once, for they were in attitudes which suggested that they had been working together to push the boat down into the river. Mr. Tanimoto lifted them away from the boat, and as he did so, he experienced such horror at disturbing the dead—preventing them, he momentarily felt, from launching their craft and going on their ghostly way—that he said out loud, " Please forgive me for taking this boat. I must use it for others, who are alive." The punt was heavy, but he managed to slide it into the water. There were no oars, and all he could find for propulsion was a thick bamboo pole. He worked the boat upstream to the most crowded part of the park and began to ferry the wounded. He could pack ten or twelve into the boat for each crossing, but as the river was too deep in the centre to pole his way across, he had to paddle with the bamboo, and consequently each trip took a very long time. He worked several hours that way.

Early in the afternoon, the fire swept into the woods of Asano Park. The first Mr. Tanimoto knew of it was when, returning in his boat, he saw that a great number of people had moved toward the riverside. On touching the bank, he went up to investigate, and when he saw the fire, he shouted, "All the young men who are not badly hurt come with me !" Father Kleinsorge moved Father Schiffer and Father LaSalle close to the edge of the river and asked people there to get them across if the fire came too near, and then joined Tanimoto's volunteers. Mr. Tanimoto sent some to look for buckets and basins and told others to beat the burning underbrush with their clothes ; when utensils were at hand, he formed a bucket chain from one of the pools in the rock gardens. The team fought the fire for more than two hours, and gradually defeated the flames. As Mr. Tanimoto's men worked, the frightened people in the park pressed closer and closer to the river, and finally the mob began to force some of the unfortunates who were on the very bank into the water. Among those driven into the river and drowned were Mrs. Matsumoto, of the Methodist School, and her daughter.

When Father Kleinsorge got back after fighting the fire, he found Father Schiffer still bleeding and terribly pale. Some Japanese stood around and stared at him, and Father Schiffer whispered, with a weak smile, "It is as if I were already dead." "Not yet," Father Kleinsorge said. He had brought Dr. Fujii's first-aid kit with him, and he had noticed Dr. Kanda in the crowd, so he sought him out and asked him if he would dress Father Schiffer's bad cuts. Dr. Kanda had seen his wife and daughter dead in the ruins of his hospital; he sat now with his head in his hands. " I can't do anything," he said. Father Kleinsorge bound more bandage around Father Schiffer's head, moved him to a steep place, and settled him so that his head was high, and soon the bleeding diminished.

The roar of approaching planes was heard about this time. Someone in the crowd near the Nakamura family shouted, " It's some Grummans coming to strafe us !" A baker named Nakashima stood up and commanded, " Everyone who is wearing anything white, take it off." Mrs. Nakamura took the blouses off her children, and opened her umbrella and made them get under it. A great number of people, even

badly burned ónes, crawled into bushes and stayed
there until the hum, evidently of a reconnaissance or
weather run, died away.

It began to rain. Mrs. Nakamura kept her children
under the umbrella. The drops grew abnormally
large and someone shouted, " The Americans are
dropping gasoline. They're going to set fire to us ! "
(This alarm stemmed from one of the theories being
passed through the park as to why so much of Hiroshima had burned: it was that a single plane had
sprayed gasoline on the city and then somehow set
fire to it in one flashing moment.)   But the drops were
palpably water, and as they fell, the wind grew stronger
and stronger, and suddenly—probably because of the
tremendous convection set up by the blazing city—a
whirlwind ripped through the park. Huge trees
crashed down; small ones were uprooted and flew
into the air. Higher, a wild array of flat things
revolved in the twisting funnel—pieces of iron roofing,
papers, doors, strips of matting. Father Kleinsorge
put a piece of cloth over Father Schiffer's eyes, so that
the feeble man would not think he was going crazy.
The gale blew Mrs. Murata, the mission housekeeper,
who was sitting close by the river, down the embank-
ment at a shallow, rocky place, and she came out with
her bare feet bloody. The vortex moved out on
to the river, where it sucked up a waterspout and
eventually spent itself.

After the storm, Mr. Tanimoto began ferrying
people again, and Father Kleinsorge asked the theological student to go across and make his way out to
the Jesuit Novitiate at Nagatsuka, about three miles

from the centre of town, and to request the priests there to come with help for Fathers Schiffer and LaSalle. The student got into Mr. Tanimoto's boat and went off with him. Father Kleinsorge asked Mrs. Nakamura if she would like to go out to Nagatsuka with the priests when they came. She said she had some luggage and her children were sick—they were still vomiting from time to time, and so, for that matter, was she—and therefore she feared she could not. He said he thought the fathers from the Novitiate could come back the next day with a pushcart to get her.

Late in the afternoon, when he went ashore for a while, Mr. Tanimoto, upon whose energy and initiative many had come to depend, heard people begging for food. He consulted Father Kleinsorge, and they decided to go back into town to get some rice from Mr. Tanimoto's Neighbourhood Association shelter and from a mission shelter. Father Cieslik and two or three others went with them. At first, when they got among the rows of prostrate houses, they did not know where they were; the change was too sudden, from a busy city of two hundred and forty-five thousand that morning to a mere pattern of residue in the afternoon. The asphalt of the streets was still so soft and hot from the fires that walking was uncomfortable. They encountered only one person, a woman, who said to them as they passed, " My husband is in those ashes." At the mission, where Mr. Tanimoto left the party, Father Kleinsorge was dismayed to see the building razed. In the garden on the way to the shelter, he noticed a pumpkin roasted on the vine.

He and Father Cieslik tasted it and it was good. They
were surprised at their hunger, and they ate quite a bit.
They got out several bags of rice and gathered up
several other cooked pumpkins and dug up some
potatoes that were nicely baked under the ground,
and started back. Mr. Tanimoto rejoined them on
the way. One of the people with him had some
cooking utensils. In the park, Mr. Tanimoto organ-
ised the lightly wounded women of his neighbourhood
to cook. Father Kleinsorge offered the Nakamura
family some pumpkin, and they tried it, but they
could not keep it on their stomachs. Altogether,
the rice was enough to feed nearly a hundred people.

Just before dark, Mr. Tanimoto came across a
twenty-year-old girl, Mrs. Kamai, the Tanimotos'
next-door neighbour. She was crouching on the
ground with the body of her infant daughter in her
arms. The baby had evidently been dead all day.
Mrs. Kamai jumped up when she saw Mr. Tanimoto
and said, " Would you please try to locate my
husband ? "

Mr. Tanimoto knew that her husband had been
inducted into the Army just the day before; he and
Mrs. Tanimoto had entertained Mrs. Kamai in the
afternoon, to make her forget. Kamai had reported
to the Chugoku Regional Army Headquarters—near
the ancient castle in the middle of town—where some
four thousand troops were stationed. Judging by the
many maimed soldiers Mr. Tanimoto had seen during
the day, he surmised that the barracks had been badly
damaged by whatever it was that had hit Hiroshima.
He knew he hadn't a chance of finding Mrs. Kamai's

husband, even if he searched, but he wanted to humour her. " I'll try," he said.

" You've got to find him," she said. " He loved our baby so much. I want him to see her once more."

III

DETAILS ARE BEING INVESTIGATED

EARLY in the evening of the day the bomb exploded, a Japanese naval launch moved slowly up and down the seven rivers of Hiroshima. It stopped here and there to make an announcement—alongside the crowded sandspits, on which hundreds of wounded lay; at the bridges, on which others were crowded; and eventually, as twilight fell, opposite Asano Park. A young officer stood up in the launch and shouted through a megaphone, "Be patient! A naval hospital ship is coming to take care of you!" The sight of the shipshape launch against the background of the havoc across the river; the unruffled young man in his neat uniform; above all, the promise of medical help— the first word of possible succour anyone had heard in nearly twelve awful hours—cheered the people in the park tremendously. Mrs. Nakamura settled her family for the night with the assurance that a doctor would come and stop their retching. Mr. Tanimoto resumed ferrying the wounded across the river. Father Kleinsorge lay down and said the Lord's Prayer and a Hail Mary to himself, and fell right asleep; but no sooner had he dropped off than Mrs. Murata, the conscientious mission housekeeper, shook him and said, "Father Kleinsorge: Did you remember to repeat your evening prayers?" He answered rather grumpily, "Of course," and he tried to go back to sleep but could not. This, apparently, was just what Mrs. Murata wanted. She began to chat with the exhausted priest. One of the questions she raised was when he thought the priests from the Novitiate, for whom he had sent a messenger in mid-afternoon, would arrive to evacuate Father Superior LaSalle and Father Schiffer.

The messenger Father Kleinsorge had sent—the theological student who had been living at the mission house—had arrived at the Novitiate, in the hills about three miles out, at half-past four. The sixteen priests there had been doing rescue work in the outskirts; they had worried about their colleagues in the city but had not known how or where to look for them. Now they hastily made two litters out of poles and boards, 'and the student led half a dozen of them back into the devastated area. They worked their way along the Ota above the city; twice the heat of the fire forced them into the river. At Misasa Bridge, they encountered a long line of soldiers making a bizarre forced march away from the the Chugoku Regional Army Headquarters in the centre of the town. All were grotesquely burned and they supported themselves with staves or leaned on one another. Sick, burned horses, hanging their heads, stood on the bridge. When the rescue party reached the park it was after dark, and progress was made extremely difficult by the tangle of fallen trees of all sizes that had been knocked down by the whirlwind that afternoon. At last—not long after Mrs. Murata asked her question—they reached their friends, and gave them wine and strong tea.

The priests discussed how to get Father Schiffer and Father LaSalle out to the Novitiate. They were afraid that blundering through the park with them would jar them too much on the wooden litters, and that the wounded men would lose too much blood. Father Kleinsorge thought of Mr. Tanimoto and his boat, and called out to him on the river. When Mr. Tanimoto reached the bank, he said he would be glad to take the injured priests and their bearers upstream to where they could find a clear roadway. The rescuers put Father Schiffer on to one of the stretchers and lowered it into the boat, and two of them went aboard with it. Mr. Tanimoto, who still had no oars, poled the punt upstream.

About half an hour later, Mr. Tanimoto came back and excitedly asked the remaining priests to help him rescue two children he had seen standing up to their shoulders in the river. A group went out and picked them up—two young girls who had lost their family and were both badly burned. The priests stretched them on the ground next to Father Kleinsorge and then embarked Father LaSalle. Father Cieslik thought he could make it out to the Novitiate on foot, so he went aboard with the others. Father Kleinsorge was too feeble; he decided to wait in the park until the next day. He asked the men to come back with a handcart, so that they could take Mrs. Nakamura and her sick children to the Novitiate.

Mr. Tanimoto shoved off again. As the boat load of priests moved slowly upstream, they heard weak cries for help. A woman's voice stood out especially: " There are people here about to be drowned ! Help us ! The water is rising ! " The sounds came from one of the sandspits, and those in the punt could see, in the reflected light of the still-burning fires, a number of wounded people lying at the edge of the river, already partly covered by the flooding tide. Mr. Tanimoto wanted to help them, but the priests were afraid that Father Schiffer would die if they didn't hurry, and they urged their ferryman along. He dropped them where he had put Father Schiffer down and then started back alone toward the sandspit.

The night was hot, and it seemed even hotter because of the fires against the sky, but the younger of the two girls Mr. Tanimoto and the priests had rescued complained to Father Kleinsorge that she was cold. He covered her with his jacket. She and her older sister had been in the salt water of the river for a couple of hours before being rescued. The younger one had huge, raw flash burns on her body; the salt water must have been excruciatingly painful to her. She began to shiver heavily, and again said it was cold. Father Kleinsorge borrowed a blanket from someone nearby and wrapped her up, but she shook more and more, and said again, " I am so cold," and then she suddenly stopped shivering and was dead.

Mr. Tanimoto found about twenty men and women on the sandspit. He drove the boat on to the bank and urged them to get aboard. They did not move and he realised that they were too weak to lift themselves. He reached down and took a woman by the hands, but her skin slipped off in huge, glove-like pieces. He was so sickened by this that he had to sit down for a moment. Then he got out into the water and, though a small man, lifted several of the men and, women, who were naked, into his boat. Their backs and breasts were clammy, and he remembered uneasily what the great burns he had seen during the day had been like: yellow at first, then red and swollen, with the skin sloughed off, and finally, in the evening, suppurated and smelly. With the tide risen, his bamboo pole was now too short and he had to paddle most of the way across with it. On the other side, at a higher spit, he lifted the slimy living bodies out and carried them up the slope away from the tide. He had to keep consciously repeating to himself, " These are human beings." It took him three trips to get them all across the river. When he had finished, he decided he had to have a rest, and he went back to the park.

As Mr. Tanimoto stepped up the dark bank, he tripped over someone, and someone else said angrily, " Look out ! That's my hand." Mr. Tanimoto, ashamed of hurting wounded people, embarrassed at being able to walk upright, suddenly thought of the naval hospital ship, which had not come (it never did), and he had for a moment a feeling of blind, murderous rage at the crew of the ship, and then at all doctors. Why didn't they come to help these people ?

Dr. Fujii lay in dreadful pain throughout the night on the floor of his family's roofless house on the edge of the city. By the light of a lantern, he had examined himself and found: left clavicle fractured; multiple abrasions and lacerations of face and body, including deep cuts on the chin, back, and legs; extensive contusions on chest and trunk; a couple of ribs possibly fractured. Had he not been so badly hurt, he might have been at Asano Park, assisting the wounded.

By nightfall, ten thousand victims of the explosion had invaded the Red Cross Hospital, and Dr. Sasaki, worn out, was moving aimlessly and dully up and down the stinking corridors with wads of bandage and bottles of mercurochrome, still wearing the glasses he had taken from the wounded nurse, binding up the worst cuts as he came to them. Other doctors were putting compresses of saline solution on the worst burns. That was all they could do. After dark, they worked by the light of the city's fires and by candles the ten remaining nurses held for them. Dr. Sasaki had not looked outside the hospital all day; the scene inside was so terrible and so compelling that it had not occurred to him to ask any questions about what had happened beyond the windows and doors. Ceilings and partitions had fallen; plaster, dust, blood, and vomit were everywhere. Patients were dying by the hundreds, but there was nobody to carry away the corpses. Some of the hospital staff distributed biscuits and rice balls, but the charnel-house smell was so strong that few were hungry. By three o'clock the next morning after nineteen straight hours of his gruesome work, Dr. Sasaki was incapable of dressing another wound. He and some other survivors of the hospital staff got straw mats and went outdoors—thousands of patients and hundreds of dead were in the yard and on the drive way — and hurried around behind the hospital and lay down in hiding to snatch some sleep. But within an hour wounded people had found them; a complaining circle formed around them: " Doctors ! Help us ! How can you sleep ? " Dr. Sasaki got up again and went back to work. Early in the day, he thought for the first time of his mother at their country home in Mukaihara, thirty miles from town. He usually went home every night. He was afraid she would think he was dead.

Near the spot up river to which Mr. Tanimoto had transported the priests, there sat a large case of rice cakes which a rescue party had evidently brought for the wounded lying thereabouts but hadn't distributed. Before evacuating the wounded priests, the others passed the cakes around and helped themselves. A few minutes later, a band of soldiers came up, and an officer, hearing the priests speaking a foreign language, drew his sword and hysterically asked who they were. One of the priests calmed him down and explained that they were Germans—allies. The officer apologised and said that there were reports going round that American parachutists had landed.

The priests decided that they should take Father Schiffer first. As they prepared to leave, Father Superior LaSalle said he felt awfully cold. One of the Jesuits gave up his coat, another his shirt; they were glad to wear less in the muggy night. The stretcher bearers started out. The theological student led the way and tried to warn the others of obstacles, but one of the priests got a foot tangled in some telephone wire and tripped and dropped his corner of the litter. Father Schiffer rolled off, lost consciousness, came to, and then vomited. The bearers picked him up and went on with him to the edge of the city, where they had arranged to meet a relay of other priests, left him with them, and turned back and got the Father Superior.

The wooden litter must have been terribly painful for Father LaSalle, in whose back scores of tiny particles of window glass were embedded. Near the edge of town, the group had to walk around an automobile burned and squatting on the narrow road, and the bearers on one side, unable to see their way in the darkness, fell into a deep ditch. Father LaSalle was thrown onto the ground and the litter broke in two. One priest went ahead to get a handcart from the Novitiate, but he soon found one beside an empty house and wheeled it back. The priests lifted Father LaSalle into the cart and pushed him over the bumpy road the rest of the way. The rector of the Novitiate, who had been a doctor before he entered the religious order, cleaned the wounds of the two priests and put them to bed between clean sheets, and they thanked God for the care they had received.

Thousands of people had nobody to help them. Miss Sasaki was one of them. Abandoned and helpless, under the crude lean-to in the courtyard of the tin factory, beside the woman who had lost a breast and the man whose burned face was scarcely a face any more, she suffered awfully that night from the pain in her broken leg. She did not sleep at all; neither did she converse with her sleepless companions.

In the park, Mrs. Murata kept Father Kleinsorge awake all night by talking to him. None of the Nakamura family were able to sleep, either; the children, in spite of being very sick, were interested in everything that happened. They were delighted when one of the city's gas-storage tanks went up in a tremendous burst of flame. Toshio, the boy, shouted to the others to look at the reflection in the river. Mr. Tanimoto, after his long run and his many hours of rescue work, dozed uneasily. When he awoke, in the first light of dawn, he looked across the river and saw that he had not carried the festered, limp bodies high enough on the sandspit the night before. The tide had risen above where he had put them; they had not had the strength to move; they must have drowned. He saw a number of bodies floating in the river.

Early that day, August 7th, the Japanese radio broadcast for the first time a succinct announcement that very few, if any, of the people most concerned with its content, the survivors in Hiroshima, happened to hear: "Hiroshima suffered considerable damage as the result of an attack by a few B-29s. It is believed that a new type of bomb was used. The details are being investigated." Nor is it probable that any of the survivors happened to be tuned in on a short-wave rebroadcast of an extraordinary announcement by the President of the United States, which identified the new bomb as atomic: "That bomb had more power than twenty thousand tons of T.N.T. It had more than two thousand times the blast power of the British Grand Slam, which is the largest bomb ever yet used in the history of warfare." Those victims who were able to worry at all about what had happened thought of it and discussed it in more primitive, childish terms—gasoline sprinkled from an aeroplane, maybe, or some combustible gas, or a big cluster of incendiaries, or the work of parachutists; but, even if they had known the truth, most of them were too

busy or too weary or too badly hurt to care that they
were the objects of the first great experiment in the use
of atomic power, which (as the voices on the short
wave shouted) no country except the United States,
with its industrial know-how, its willingness to throw
two billion gold dollars into an important wartime
gamble, could possibly have developed.

Mr. Tanimoto was still angry at doctors. He decided
that he would personally bring one to Asano Park—
by the scruff of the neck, if necessary. He crossed the
river, went past the Shinto shrine where he had met his
wife for a brief moment the day before, and walked
to the East Parade Ground. Since this had long
before been designated as an evacuation area, he
thought he would find an aid station there. He did
find one, operated by an Army medical unit, but he
also saw that its doctors were hopelessly overburdened,
with thousands of patients sprawled among corpses
across the field in front of it. Nevertheless, he went
up to one of the army doctors and said, as reproach-
fully as he could, " Why have you not come to Asano
Park ? You are badly needed there."

Without even looking up from his work, the doctor
said in a tired voice, " This is my station."

" But there are many dying on the river bank over
there."

" The first duty," the doctor said, " is to take care
of the slightly wounded."

" Why—when there are many who are heavily
wounded on the river-bank ? "

The doctor moved to another patient. " In an
emergency like this." he said, as if he were reciting

from a manual, " the first task is to help as many
as possible—to save as many lives as possible. There
is no hope for the heavily wounded. They will die.
We can't bother with them."

" That might be right from a medical standpoint—'
Mr. Tanimoto began, but then he looked out across
the field, where the many dead lay close and intimate
with those who were still living, and he turned away
without finishing his sentence, angry now with himself.
He didn't know what to do; he had promised some of
the dying people in the park that he would bring
medical aid. They might die feeling cheated. He
saw a ration stand at one side of the field, and he went
to it and begged some rice and biscuits, and he took
them back, in lieu of doctors, to the people in the
park.

The morning, again, was hot. Father Kleinsorge
went to fetch water for the wounded in a bottle and a
teapot he had borrowed. He had heard that it was
possible to get fresh tap water outside Asano Park.
Going through the rock gardens, he had to climb over
and crawl under the trunks of fallen pine trees; he
found he was weak. There were many dead in the
gardens. At a beautiful moon bridge, he passed a
naked living woman who seemed to have been burned
from head to toe and was red all over. Near the
entrance to the park, an Army doctor was working,
but the only medicine he had was iodine, which he
painted over cuts, bruises, slimy burns, everything—
and by now everything that he had painted had pus on
it. Outside the gate of the park, Father Kleinsorge
found a faucet that still worked—part of the plumbing

of a vanished house—and he filled his vessels and returned. When he had given the wounded the water, he made a second trip. This time, the woman by the bridge was dead. On his way back with the water, he got lost on a detour around a fallen tree, and as he looked for his way through the woods, he heard a voice ask from the underbrush, " Have you anything to drink ? " He saw a uniform. Thinking there was just one soldier, he approached with the water. When he had penetrated the bushes, he saw there were about twenty men, and they were all in exactly the same nightmarish state: their faces were wholly burned, their eyesockets were hollow, the fluid from their melted eyes had run down their cheeks. (They must have had their faces upturned when the bomb went off; perhaps they were anti-aircraft personnel.) Their mouths were mere swollen, pus-covered wounds, which they could not bear to stretch enough to admit the spout of the teapot. So Father Kleinsorge got a large piece of grass and drew out the stem so as to make a straw, and gave them all water to drink that way. One of them said, " I can't see anything." Father Kleinsorge answered as cheerfully as he could, " There's a doctor at the entrance to the park. He's busy now, but he'll come soon and fix your eyes, I hope."

Since that day, Father Kleinsorge has thought back to how queasy he had once been at the sight of pain, how someone else's cut finger used to make him turn faint. Yet there in the park he was so benumbed that immediately after leaving this horrible sight he stopped on a path by one of the pools and discussed with a lightly wounded man whether it would be safe to eat

the fat, two-foot carp that floated dead on the surface
of the water.   They decided, after some consideration,
that it would be unwise.

Father Kleinsorge filled the containers a third time
and went back to the river-bank.   There, amid the dead
and dying, he saw a young woman with a needle and
thread mending her kimono, which had been slightly
torn.   Father   Kleinsorge   joshed   her.   " My,   but
you're a dandy ! " he said.   She laughed.

He felt tired and lay down.   He began to talk with
two engaging children whose acquaintance he had
made the afternoon before.   He learned that their
name was Kataoka; the girl was thirteen, the boy
five.   The girl had been just about to set out for a
barber shop when the bomb fell.   As the family
started for Asano Park, their mother decided to turn
back for some food and extra clothing; they became
separated from her in the crowd of fleeing people,
and they had not seen her since.   Occasionally they
stopped suddenly in their perfectly cheerful playing
and began to cry for their mother.

It was difficult for all the children in the park to
sustain the sense of tragedy.   Toshio Nakamura got
quite excited when he saw his friend Seichi Sato riding
up the river in a boat with his family, and he ran to the
bank and waved and shouted, " Sato !   Sato ! "

The boy turned his head and shouted, " Who's
that ? "

" Nakamura."

" Hello, Toshio ! "

" Are you all safe ? "

" Yes.   What about you ? "

" Yes, we're all right. My sisters are vomiting, but I'm fine."

Father Kleinsorge began to be thirsty in the dreadful heat, and he did not feel strong enough to go for water again. A little before noon, he saw a Japanese woman handing something out. Soon she came to him and said in a kindly voice, " These are tea leaves. Chew them, young man, and you won't feel thirsty." The woman's gentleness made Father Kleinsorge suddenly want to cry. For weeks, he had been feeling oppressed by the hatred of foreigners that the Japanese seemed increasingly to show, and he had been uneasy even with his Japanese friends. This stranger's gesture made him a little hysterical.

Around noon, the priests arrived from the Novitiate with the handcart. They had been to the site of the mission house in the city and had retrieved some suitcases that had been stored in the air-raid shelter and had also picked up the remains of melted holy vessels in the ashes of the chapel. They now packed Father Kleinsorge's papier-maché suitcase and the things belonging to Mrs. Murata and the Nakamuras into the cart, put the two Nakamura girls aboard, and prepared to start out. Then one of the Jesuits who had a practical turn of mind remembered that they had been notified some time before that if they suffered property damage at the hands of the enemy, they could enter a claim for compensation with the prefectural police. The holy men discussed this matter there in the park, with the wounded as silent as the dead around them, and decided that Father Kleinsorge, as a former resident of the destroyed mission, was the one to enter the claim. So, as the others went off with the handcart, Father Kleinsorge said good-bye to the Kataoka children and trudged to a police station. Fresh, clean-uniformed policemen from another town were in charge, and a crowd of dirty and disarrayed citizens crowded around them, mostly asking after lost relatives. Father Kleinsorge filled out a claim form and started walking through the centre of town on his way to Nagatsuka. It was then that he first realised the extent of the damage; he passed block after block of ruins, and even after all he had seen in the park, his breath was taken away. By the time he reached the Novitiate, he was sick with exhaustion. The last thing he did as he fell into bed was request that someone go back for the motherless Kataoka children.

Altogether, Miss Sasaki was left two days and two nights under the piece of propped-up roofing with her crushed leg and her two unpleasant comrades. Her only diversion was when men came to the factory air-raid shelters, which she could see from under one corner of her shelter, and hauled corpses up out of them with ropes. Her leg became discoloured, swollen, and putrid. All that time, she went without food and water. On the third day, August 8th, some friends who supposed she was dead came to look for her body and found her. They told her that her mother, father, and baby brother, who at the time of the explosion were in the Tamura Pediatric Hospital, where the baby was a patient, had all been given up as certainly dead, since the hospital was totally destroyed. Her friends then left her to think that piece of news over. Later, some men picked her up by the arms and legs and carried her quite a distance to a truck. For about an hour, the truck moved over a bumpy road, and Miss Sasaki, who had become convinced that she was dulled to pain, discovered that she was not. The men lifted her out at a relief station in the section of Inokuchi, where two Army doctors looked at her. The moment one of them touched her wound, she fainted. She came to in to hear them discuss whether or not to cut off her leg; one said there was gas gangrene in the lips of the wound and predicted she would die unless they amputated, and the other said that was too bad, because they had no equipment with which to do the job. She fainted again. When she recovered consciousness, she was being carried somewhere on a stretcher. She was put aboard a launch, which went to the nearby island of Ninoshima, and she was taken to a military hospital there. Another doctor examined her and said that she did not have gas gangrene, though she did have a fairly ugly compound fracture. He said quite coldly that he was sorry, but this was a hospital for operative surgical cases only, and because she had no gangrene she would have to return to Hiroshima that night. But then the doctor took her temperature and what he saw on the thermometer made him decide to let her stay

That day, August 8th, Father Cieslik went into the city to look for Mr. Fukai, the Jananese secretary of the diocese, who had ridden unwillingly out or the flaming city on Father Kleinsorge's nack and then had run hack crazily into it. Father Cieslik started hunting in the neighbourhood of Sakai Bridge, where the Jesuits had last seen Mr. Fukai; he went to the East Parade Ground, the evacuation area to which the secretary might have gone, and looked for him among the wounded and dead there; he went to the prefectural police and made inquiries. He could not find any trace of the man. Back at the Novitiate that evening, the theological student, who had been rooming with Mr. Fukai at the mission house, told the priests that the secretary had remarked to him, during an air-raid alarm one day not long before the bombing, "Japan is dying. If there is a real air raid here in Hiroshima, I want to die with our country." The priests concluded that Mr. Fukai had run back to immolate himself in the flames. They never saw him again.

At the Red Cross Hospital, Dr. Sasaki worked for three straight days with only one hour's sleep. On the second day, he began to sew up the worst cuts, and right through the following night and all the next day he stitched. Many of the wounds were festered. Fortunately, someone had found intact a supply of *narucopon* a Japanese sedative, and he gave it to many who were in pain. Word went around among the staff that there must have been something peculiar about the great bomb, because on the second day the vice-chief of the hospital went down in the basement to the vault where the X-ray plates were stored and found the whole stock exposed as they lay. That day, a fresh doctor and ten nurses came in from the city of Yamaguchi with extra bandages and antiseptics, and the third day another physician and a dozen more nurses arrived from Matsue—yet there were still only eight doctors for ten thousand patients. In the afternoon of the third day, exhausted from his foul tailoring, Dr. Sasaki became obsessed with the idea that his mother thought he was dead. He got permission to go to Mukaihara. He walked out to the first suburbs, beyond which the electric train service was still functioning, and reached home late in the evening. His mother said she had known he was all right all along; a wounded nurse had stopped by to tell her. He went to bed and slept for seventeen hours.

Before dawn on August 8th, sómeone entered the room at the Novitiate where Father Kleinsorge was in bed, reached up to the hanging light bulb, and switched it on. The sudden flood of light, pouring in on Father Kleinsorge's half sleep, brought him leaping out of bed, braced for a new concussion. When he realised what had happened, he laughed confusedly and went back to bed. He stayed there all day.

On August 9th, Father Kleinsorge was still tired. The rector looked at his cuts and said they were not even worth dressing, and if Father Kleinsorge kept them clean, they would heal in three or four days. Father Kleinsorge felt uneasy; he could not yet comprehend what he had been through; as if he were guilty of something awful, he felt he had to go back to the scene of the violence he had experienced. He got up out of bed and walked into the city. He scratched for a while in the ruins of the mission house, but he found nothing. He went to the sites of a couple of schools and asked after people he knew. He looked for some of the city's Japanese Catholics, but he found only fallen houses. He walked back to the Novitiate, stupefied and without any new understanding.

At two minutes after eleven o'clock on the morning of August 9th, the second atomic bomb was dropped, on Nagasaki. It was several days before the survivors of Hiroshima knew they had company, because the Japanese radio and newspapers were being extremely cautious on the subject of the strange weapon.

On August 9th, Mr. Tanimoto was still working in the park. He went to the suburb of Ushida, where his wife was staying with friends, and got a tent which he had stored there before the bombing. He now took it to the park and set it up as a shelter for some of the wounded who could not move or be moved. Whatever he did in the park, he felt he was being watched by the twenty-year-old girl, Mrs. Kamai, his former neighbour, whom he had seen on the day the bomb exploded, with her dead baby daughter in her arms. She kept the small corpse in her arms for four days, even though it began smelling bad on the second day. Once, Mr. Tanimoto sat with her for a while, and she told him that the bomb had buried her under their house with the baby strapped to her back, and that when she had dug herself free, she had discovered that the baby was choking, its mouth full of dirt. With her little finger, she had carefully cleaned out the infant's mouth, and for a time the child had breathed normally and seemed all right; then suddenly it had died. Mrs. Kamai also talked about what a fine man her husband was, and again urged Mr. Tanimoto to search for him. Since Mr. Tanimoto had been all through the city the first day and had seen terribly burned soldiers from Kamai's post, the Chugoku Regional Army Headquarters, everywhere, he knew it would be impossible to find Kamai, even if he were living, but of course, he didn't tell her that.   Every time she saw Mr. Tanimoto, she asked whether he had found her husband.   Once, he tried to suggest that perhaps it was time to cremate the baby, but Mrs. Kamai only held it tighter.   He began to keep away from her, but whenever he looked at her, she was staring at him and her eyes asked the same question.   He tried to escape her glance by keeping his back turned to her as much as possible.

The Jesuits took about fifty refugees into the exquisite chapel of the Novitiate.   The rector gave them what medical care he could—mostly just the cleaning away of pus.   Each of the Nakamuras was provided with a blanket and mosquito net.   Mrs. Nakamura and her younger daughter had no appetite and ate nothing; her son and other daughter ate, and lost, each meal they were offered.   On August 10th, a friend, Mrs. Osaki, came to see them and told them that her son Hideo had been burned alive in the factory where he worked.   This Hideo had been a kind of hero to Toshio, who had often gone to the plant to watch him run his machine.   That night, Toshio woke up screaming.   He had dreamed that he had seen Mrs. Osaki coming out of an opening in the ground with her family, and then he saw Hideo at his machine, a big one with a revolving belt, and he himself was standing beside Hideo, and for some reason this was terrifying

On August 10th, Father Kleinsorge, having heard from someone that Dr. Fujii had been injured and that he had eventually gone to the summer house of a friend of his named Okuma, in the village of Fukawa, asked Father Cieslik if he would go and see how Dr. Fujii was. Father Cieslik went to Misasa station, outside Hiroshima, rode for twenty minutes on an electric train, and then walked for an hour and a half in a terribly hot sun to Mr. Okuma's house, which was beside the Ota River at the foot of a mountain. He found Dr. Fujii sitting in a chair in a kimono, applying compresses to his broken collar-bone. The Doctor told Father Cieslik about having lost his glasses and said that his eyes bothered him. He showed the priest huge blue and green stripes where beams had bruised him. He offered the Jesuit first a cigarette and then whisky, though it was only eleven in the morning. Father Cieslik thought it would please Dr. Fujii if he took a little, so he said yes. A servant brought some Suntory whisky, and the Jesuit, the Doctor, and the host had a very pleasant chat. Mr. Okuma had lived in Hawaii, and he told some things about Americans. Dr. Fujii talked a bit about the disaster. He said that Mr. Okuma and a nurse had gone into the ruins of his hospital and brought back a small safe which he had moved into his air-raid shelter. This contained some surgical instruments, and Dr. Fujii gave Father Cieslik a few pairs of scissors and tweezers for the rector at the Novitiate. Father Cieslik was bursting with some inside dope he had, but he waited until the conversation turned naturally to the mystery of the bomb. Then he said he knew what kind of a bomb it was; he had the secret on the best authority— that of a Japanese newspaperman who had dropped in at the Novitiate. The bomb was not a bomb at all; it was a kind of fine magnesium powder sprayed over the whole city by a single plane, and it exploded when it came into contact with the live wires of the city power system. "That means," said Dr. Fujii, perfectly satisfied, since after all the information came from a newspaperman, "that it can only be dropped on big cities and only in the daytime, when the tram lines and so forth are in operation."

After five days of ministering to the wounded in the park, Mr. Tanimoto returned, on August 11th, to his parsonage and dug around in the ruins. He retrieved some diaries and church records that had been kept in books and were only charred around the edges, as well as some cooking utensils and pottery. While he was at work, a Miss Tanaka came and said that her father had been asking for him. Mr. Tanimoto had reason to hate her father, the retired shipping-company official who, though he made a great show of his charity, was notoriously selfish and cruel, and who, just a few days before the bombing, had said openly to several people that Mr. Tanimoto was a spy for the Americans. Several times he had derided Christianity and called it un-Japanese. At the moment of the bombing, Mr. Tanaka had been walking in the street in front of the city's radio station. He received serious flash burns, but he was able to walk home. He took refuge in his Neighbourhood Association shelter and from there tried hard to get medical aid. He expected all the doctors of Hiroshima to come to him, because he was so rich and so famous for giving his money away. When none of them came, he angrily set out to look for them; leaning on his daughter's arm, he walked from private hospital to private hospital, but all were in ruins, and he went back and lay down in the shelter again. Now he was very weak and knew he was going to die. He was willing to be comforted by any religion.

Mr. Tanimoto went to help him. He descended into the tomblike shelter and, when his eyes were adjusted to the darkness, saw Mr. Tanaka, his face and arms puffed up and covered with pus and blood, and his eyes swollen shut. The old man smelled very bad, and he moaned constantly. He seemed to recognise Mr. Tanimoto's voice. Standing at the shelter stairway to get light, Mr. Tanimoto read loudly from a Japanese-language pocket Bible : " For a thousand years in Thy sight are but as yesterday when it is past, and as a watch in the night. Thou carriest the children of men away as with a flood ; they are as a sleep ; in the morning they are like grass which groweth up. In the morning it flourisheth and groweth up ; in the evening it is cut down, and withereth. For we are consumed by Thine anger and by Thy wrath are we troubled. Thou hast set our iniquities before Thee, our secret sins in the light of Thy countenance. For all our days are passed away in Thy wrath: we spend our years as a tale that is told . . . ."

Mr. Tanaka died as Mr. Tanimoto read the psalm.

On August 11th, word came to the Ninoshima

Military Hospital that a large number of casualties from the Chugoku Regional Army Headquarters were to arrive on the island that day, and it was deemed necessary to evacuate all civilian patients. Miss Sasaki, still running an alarmingly high fever, was put on a large ship. She lay out on deck, with a pillow under her leg. There were awnings over the deck but the vessel's course put her in the sunlight. She felt as if she were under a magnifying glass in the sun. Pus oozed out of her wound, and soon the whole pillow was covered with it. She was taken ashore at Hatsukaichi, a town several miles to the south-west of Hiroshima, and put in the Goddess of Mercy Primary School, which had been turned into a hospital. She lay there several days before a specialist on fractures came from Kobe. By then her leg was red and swollen up to her hip. The doctor decided he could not set the breaks. He made an incision and put in a rubber pipe to drain off the putrescence.

At the Novitiate, the motherless Kataoka children were inconsolable. Father Cieslik worked hard to keep them distracted. He put riddles to them. He asked, " What is the cleverest animal in the world ? " and after the thirteen-year-old girl had guessed the ape, the elephant, the horse, he said, " No, it must be the hippopotamus," because in Japanese that animal is *kaba*, the reverse of *baka*, stupid. He told Bible stories, beginning, in the order of things, with the Creation. He showed them a scrapbook of snapshots taken in Europe. Nevertheless, they cried most of the time for their mother.

Several days later, Father Cieslik started hunting

for the children's family.. First, he learned through
the police that an uncle had been to the authorities in
Kure, a city not far away, to inquire for the children,
After that, he heard that an older brother had been
trying to trace them through the post office in Ujina,
a suburb of Hiroshima. Still later, he heard that the
mother was alive and was on Goto Island, off Nagasaki.
And at last, by keeping a check on the Ujina post
office, he got in touch with the brother and returned
the children to their mother.

About a week after the bomb dropped, a vague,
incomprehensible rumour reached Hiroshima—that the
city had been destroyed by the energy released when
atoms were somehow split in two. The weapon
was referred to in this word-of-mouth report as *genshi
bakudan*—the root characters of which can be trans-
lated as " original child bomb." No one understood
the idea or put any more credence in it than in the
powdered magnesium and such things. Newspapers
were being brought in from other cities, but they were
still confining themselves to extremely general state-
ments, such as Domei's assertion on August 12th:
" There is nothing to do but admit the tremendous
power of this inhuman bomb." Already, Japanese
physicists had entered the city with Lauritsen electroscopes and Neher electrometers; they understood the
idea all too well.

On August 12th, the Nakamuras, all of them still
rather sick, went to the nearby town of Kabe and
moved in with Mrs. Nakamura's sister-in-law. The
next day, Mrs. Nakamura, although she was too ill
to walk much, returned to Hiroshima alone, by electric

car to the outskirts, by foot from there. All week, at the Novitiate, she had worried about her mother, brother, and older sister, who had lived in the part of town called Fukuro, and besides, she felt drawn by some fascination, just as Father Kleinsorge had been. She discovered that her family were all dead. She went back to Kabe so amazed and depressed by what she had seen and learned in the city that she could not speak that evening.

A comparative orderliness, at least, began to be established at the Red Cross Hospital. Dr. Sasaki, back from his rest, undertook to classify his patients (who were still scattered everywhere, even on the stairways). The staff gradually swept up the debris. Best of all, the nurses and attendants started to remove the corpses. Disposal of the dead, by decent cremation and enshrinement, is a greater moral responsibility to the Japanese than adequate care of the living. Relatives identified most of the first day's dead in and around the hospital. Beginning on the second day, whenever a patient appeared to be moribund, a piece of paper with his name on it was fastened to his clothing. The corpse detail carried the bodies to a clearing outside, placed them on pyres of wood from ruined houses, burned them, put some of the ashes in envelopes intended for exposed X-ray plates, marked the envelopes with the names of the deceased, and piled them, neatly and respectfully, in stacks in the main office. In a few days, the envelopes filled one whole side of the impromptu shrine.

In Kabe, on the morning of August 15th, ten-year-old Toshio Nakamura heard an airplane overhead. He ran outdoors and identified it with a professional eye as a B-29. " There goes Mr. B !" he shouted.

One of his relatives called out to him, " Haven't you had enough of Mr. B ?"

The question had a kind of symbolism. At almost that very moment, the dull, dispirited voice of Hirohito, the Emperor Tenno, was speaking for the first time in history over the radio: " After pondering deeply the general trends of the world and the actual conditions obtaining in Our Empire to-day, We have decided to effect a settlement of the present situation by resorting to an extraordinary measure. . . ."

Mrs. Nakamura had gone to the city again, to dig up some rice she had buried in her Neighbourhood Association air-raid shelter. She got it and started back for Kabe. On the electric car, quite by chance, she ran into her younger sister, who had not been in Hiroshima the day of the bombing. " Have you heard the news ?" her sister asked.

" What news ?"

" The war is over."

" Don't say such a foolish thing, sister."

" But I heard it over the radio myself." And then, in a whisper, " It was the Emperor's voice."

" Oh," Mrs. Nakamura said (she needed nothing more to make her give up thinking, in spite of the atomic bomb, that Japan still had a chance to win the war), " in that case . . ."

Some time later, in a letter to an American, Mr. Tanimoto described the events of that morning. " At the time of the Post-War, the marvellous thing in our history happened. Our Emperor broadcasted his own voice through radio directly to us, common people of Japan. August 15th we were told that some news of great importance could be heard and all of us should hear it. So I went to Hiroshima railway station. There set a loudspeaker in the ruins of the station. Many civilians, all of them were in boundage, some being helped by shoulder of their daughters, some sustaining their injured feet by sticks, they listened to the broadcast and when they came to realize the fact that it was the Emperor, they cried with full tears in their eyes. ' What a wonderful blessing it is that Tenno himself call on us and we can hear his own voice in person. We are thoroughly satisfied in such a great sacrifice.' When they came to know the war was ended—that is, Japan was defeated, they, of course, were deeply disappointed, but followed after their Emperor's commandment in calm spirit, making whole-hearted sacrifice for the everlasting peace of the world —and Japan started her new way."

IV

PANIC GRASS AND FEVERFEW

On August 18th, twelve days after the bomb burst, Father Kleinsorge set out on foot for Hiroshima from the Novitiate with his papier-maché suitcase in his hand. He had begun to think that this bag, in which he kept his valuables, had a talismanic quality, because of the way he had found it after the explosion, standing handle-side up in the doorway of his room, while the desk under which he had previously hidden it was in splinters all over the floor. Now he was using it to carry the yen belonging to the Society of Jesus to the Hiroshima branch of the Yokohama Specie Bank, already re-opened in its half-ruined building. On the whole, he felt quite well that morning. It is true that the minor cuts he had received had not healed in three or four days, as the rector of the Novitiate, who had examined them, had positively promised they would, but Father Kleinsorge had rested well for a week and considered that he was again ready for hard work. By now he was accustomed to the terrible scene through which he walked on his way into the city: the large rice field near the Novitiate, streaked with brown; the houses on the outskirts of the city, standing but decrepit, with broken windows and dishevelled tiles; and then, quite suddenly, the beginning of the four square miles of reddish-brown scar, where nearly everything had been buffeted. down and burned; range on range of collapsed city blocks, with here and there a crude sign erected on a pile of ashes and tiles (" Sister, where are you ?" or " All safe and we live at Toyosaka "); naked trees and canted telephone poles; the few standing, gutted buildings only accentuating the horizontality of everything else (the Museum of Science and Industry, with its dome stripped to its steel frame, as if for an autopsy; the modern Chamber of Commerce Building, its tower as cold, rigid, and unassailable after the blow as before; the huge, low-lying, camouflaged city hall; the row of dowdy banks, caricaturing a shaken economic system); and in the streets a macabre traffic—hundreds of crumpled bicycles, shells of street cars and automobiles, all halted in mid-motion. The whole way, Father Kleinsorge was oppressed by the thought that all the damage he saw had been done in one instant by one bomb. By the time he reached the centre of town, the day had become very hot. He walked to the Yokohama Bank, which was doing business in a temporary wooden stall on the ground floor of its building, deposited the money, went by the mission compound just to have another look at the wreckage, and then started back to the Novitiate. About half-way there, he began to have peculiar sensations. The more or less magical suitcase, now empty, suddenly seemed terribly heavy. His knees grew weak. He felt excruciatingly tired. With a considerable expenditure of spirit, he managed to reach the Novitiate. He did not think his weakness was worth mentioning to the other Jesuits. But a couple of days later, while attempting to say Mass, he had an onset of faintness and even after three attempts was unable to go through with the service, and the next morning the rector, who had examined Father Kleinsorge's apparently negligible but unhealed cuts daily, asked in surprise, " What have you done to your wounds ?" They had suddenly opened wider and were swollen and inflamed.

As she dressed on the morning of August 20th, in the home of her sister-in-law in Kabe, not far from Nagatsuka, Mrs. Nakamura, who had suffered no cuts or burns at all, though she had been rather nauseated all through the week she and her children had spent as guests of Father Kleinsorge and the other Catholics at the Novitiate, began fixing her hair and noticed, after one stroke, that her comb carried with it a whole handful of hair; the second time, the same thing happened, so she stopped combing at once. But in the next three or four days, her hair kept falling out of its own accord, until she was quite bald. She began living indoors, practically in hiding. On August 26th, both she and her younger daughter, Myeko, woke up feeling extremely weak and tired, and they stayed on their bedrolls. Her son and other daughter, who had shared every experience with her during and after the bombing, felt fine.

At about the same time—he lost track of the days, so hard was he working to set up a temporary place of worship in a private house he had rented in the outskirts—Mr. Tanimoto fell suddenly ill with a general malaise, weariness, and feverishness, and he, too, took to his bedroll on the floor of the half-wrecked house of a friend in the suburb of Ushida.

These four did not realise it, but they were coming down with the strange, capricious disease which came later to be known as radiation sickness.

Miss Sasaki lay in steady pain in the Goddess of

Mercy Primary School, at Hatsukaichi, the fourth station to the south-west of Hiroshima on the electric train. An internal infection still prevented the proper setting of the compound fracture of her lower left leg. A young man who was in the same hospital and who seemed to have grown fond of her in spite of her unremitting preoccupation with her suffering, or else just pitied her because of it, lent her a Japanese translation of de Maupassant, and she tried to read the stories, but she could concentrate for only four or five minutes at a time.

The hospitals and aid stations around Hiroshima were so crowded in the first weeks after the bombing, and their staffs were so variable, depending on their health and on the unpredictable arrival of outside help, that patients had to be constantly shifted from place to place. Miss Sasaki, who had already been moved three times, twice by ship, was taken at the end of August to an engineering school, also at Hatsu-kaichi. Because her leg did not improve but swelled more and more, the doctors at the school bound it with crude splints and took her by car, on September 9th, to the Red Cross Hospital in Hiroshima. This was the first chance she had had to look at the ruins of Hiroshima; the last time she had been carried through the city's streets, she had been hovering on the edge of unconsciousness. Even though the wreckage had been described to her, and though she was still in pain, the sight horrified and amazed her, and there was something she noticed about it that particularly gave her the creeps. Over everything—up through the wreckage of the city, in gutters, along the river banks, tangled among tiles and tin roofing, climbing on charred tree trunks—was a blanket of fresh, vivid, lush, optimistic green; the verdancy rose even from the foundations of ruined houses. Weeds already hid the ashes, and wild flowers were in bloom among the city's bones. The bomb had not only left the underground organs of plants intact; it had stimulated them. Everywhere were bluets and Spanish bayonets, goosefoot, morning glories and day lilies, the hairy-fruited bean, purslane and clotbur and sesame and panic grass and feverfew. Especially in a circle at the centre, sickle senna grew in extraordinary regeneration, not only standing among the charred remnants of the same plant but pushing up in new places, among bricks and through cracks in the asphalt. It actually seemed as if a load of sickle-senna seed had been dropped along with the bomb.

At the Red Cross Hospital, Miss Sasaki was put under the care of Dr. Sasaki. Now, a month after the explosion, something like order had been reestablished in the hospital; which is to say that the patients who still lay in the corridors at least had mats to sleep on and that the supply of medicines, which had given out in the first few days, had been replaced, though inadequately, by contributions from other cities. Dr. Sasaki, who had had one seventeen-hour. sleep at his home on the third night, had ever since then rested only about six hours a night, on a mat at the hospital; he had lost twenty pounds from his very small body; he still wore the ill-fitting glasses he had borrowed from an injured nurse.

Since Miss Sasaki was a woman and was so sick

(and perhaps, he afterwards admitted, just a little bit because she was named Sasaki), Dr. Sasaki put her on a mat in a semi-private room, which at that time had only eight people in it. He questioned her and put down on her record card, in the correct, scrunched-up German in which he wrote all his records: "*Mittel-grosse Patientin in gutem Ernahrungszustand. Fraktur am linken Unterschenkelknochen mit Wunde; Ansch-wellung in der linken Unterschenkelgegend. Haut und sichtbare Schleimhäute mässig durchblutet und kein Oedema*," noting that she was a medium-sized female patient in good general health; that she had a com-pound fracture of the left tibia, with swelling of the left lower leg; that her skin and visible mucous mem-branes were heavily spotted with *petechiae*, which are hemorrhages about the size of grains of rice, or even as big as soya beans; and, in addition, that her head, eyes, throat, lungs, and heart were apparently normal; and that she had a fever. He wanted to set her fracture and put her leg in a cast; but he had run out of plaster of Paris long since, so he just stretched her out on a mat and prescribed aspirin for her fever, and glucose intravenously and diastase orally for her under-nourishment (which he had not entered on her record because everyone suffered from it). She exhibited only one of the queer symptoms so many of his patients were just then beginning to show—the spot hemorr-hages.

Dr. Fujii was still pursued by bad luck, which still was connected with rivers. Now he was living in the summer house of Mr. Okuma, in Fukawa. This house clung to the steep banks of the Ota River. Here his injuries seemed to make good progress, and he even began to treat refugees who came to him from the neighbourhood, using medical supplies he had retrieved from a cache in the suburbs. He noticed in some of his patients a curious syndrome of symptoms that cropped out in the third and fourth weeks, but he was not able to do much more than swathe cuts and burns. Early in September, it began to rain, steadily and heavily. The river rose. On September 17th, there came a cloudburst and then a typhoon, and the water crept higher and higher up the bank. Mr. Okuma and Dr. Fujii became alarmed and scrambled up the mountain to a peasant's house. (Down in Hiroshima, the flood took up where the bomb had left off—swept away bridges that had survived the blast, washed out streets, undermined foundations of buildings that still stood—and ten miles to the west, the Ono Army Hospital, where a team of experts from Kyoto Imperial University was, studying the delayed affliction of the patients, suddenly slid down a beautiful, pine-dark mountainside into the Inland Sea and drowned most of the investigators and their mysteriously diseased patients alike.) After the storm, Dr. Fujii and Mr. Okuma went down to the river and found that the Okuma house had been washed altogether away.

Because so many people were suddenly feeling sick nearly a month after the atomic bomb was dropped, an unpleasant rumour began to move around, and eventually it made its way to the house in Kabe where Mrs. Nakamura lay bald and ill. It was that the atomic bomb had deposited some sort of poison on Hiroshima which would give off deadly emanations for seven years; nobody could go there all that time. This especially upset Mrs. Nakamura, who remembered that in a moment of confusion on the morning of the explosion she had literally sunk her entire means of livelihood, her Sankoku sewing machine, in the small cement water tank in front of what was left of her house; now no one would be able to go and fish it out. Up to this time, Mrs. Nakamura and her relatives had been quite resigned and passive about the moral issue of the atomic bomb, but this rumour suddenly aroused them to more hatred and resentment of America than they had felt all through the war.

Japanese physicists, who knew a great deal about atomic fission (one of them owned a cyclotron), worried about lingering radiation at Hiroshima, and in mid-August, not many days after President Truman's disclosure of the type of bomb that had been dropped, they entered the city to make investigations. The first thing they did was roughly to determine a centre by observing the side on which telephone poles all round the heart of the town were scorched; they settled on the torii gateway of the Gokoku Shrine, right next to the parade ground of the Chugoku Regional Army Headquarters. From there, they worked north and south with Lauritsen electroscopes, which are sensitive to both beta rays and gamma rays. These indicated that the highest intensity of radio-activity, near the torii, was 4.2 times the average natural " leak " of ultra-short waves for the earth of that area. The scientists noticed that the flash of the bomb had discoloured concrete to a light reddish tint, had scaled off the surface of granite, and had scorched certain other types of building material, and that consequently the bomb had, in some places, left prints of the shadows that had been cast by its light. The experts found, for instance, a permanent shadow thrown on the roof of the Chamber of Commerce Building (220 yards from the rough centre) by the structure's rectangular tower; several others in the look-out post on top of the Hypothec Bank (2,050 yards); another in the tower of the Chugoku Electric Supply Building (800 yards); another projected by the handle of a gas pump (2,630 yards); and several on granite tombstones in the Gokoku Shrine (385 yards). By triangulating these and other such shadows with the objects that formed them, the scientists determined that the exact centre was a spot a hundred and fifty yards south of the torii and a few yards south-east of the pile of ruins that had once been the Shima Hospital. (A few vague human silhouettes were found, and these gave rise to stories that eventually included fancy and precise details. One story told how a painter on a ladder was monumentalized in a kind of bas-relief on the stone facade of a bank building on which he was at work, in the act of dipping his brush into his paint can; another, how a man and his cart on the bridge near the Museum of Science and Industry, almost under the centre of the explosion, were cast down in an embossed shadow which made it clear that the man was about to whip his horse.) Starting east and west from the actual centre, the scientists, in early September, made new measurements, and the highest radiation they found this time was 3.9 times the natural " leak." Since radiation of at least a thousand times the natural

" leak " would be required to cause serious effects on the human body, the scientists announced that people could enter Hiroshima without any peril at all.

As soon as this reassurance reached the household in which Mrs. Nakamura was concealing herself—or, at any rate, within a short time after her hair had started growing back again—her whole family relaxed their extreme hatred of America, and Mrs. Nakamura sent her brother-in-law to look for the sewing machine. It was still submerged in the water tank, and when he brought it home, she saw, to her dismay, that it was all rusted and useless.

By the end of the first week in September, Father Kleinsorge was in bed at the Novitiate with a fever of 102.2, and since he seemed to be getting worse, his colleagues decided to send him to the Catholic International Hospital in Tokyo. Father Cieslik and the rector took him as far as Kobe and a Jesuit from that city took him the rest of the way, with a message from a Kobe doctor to the Mother Superior of the International Hospital: " Think twice before you give this man blood transfusions, because with atomic-bomb patients we aren't at all sure that, if you stick needles in them, they'll stop bleeding."

When Father Kleinsorge arrived at the hospital, he was terribly pale and very shaky. He complained that the bomb had upset his digestion and given him abdominal pains. His white blood count was three thousand (five to seven thousand is normal), he was seriously anaemic, and his temperature was 104. A doctor who did not know much about these strange manifestations—Father Kleinsorge was one of a handful of atomic patients who had reached Tokyo—came to see him, and to the patient's face he was most encouraging. "You'll be out of here in two weeks," he said. But when the doctor got out in the corridor, he said to the Mother Superior, "He'll die. All these bomb people die—you'll see. They go along for a couple of weeks and then they die."

The doctor prescribed suralimentation for Father Kleinsorge. Every three hours, they forced some eggs or beef juice into him, and they fed him all the sugar he could stand. They gave him vitamins, and iron pills and arsenic (in Fowler's solution) for his anaemia. He confounded both the doctor's predictions; he neither died nor got up in a fortnight. Despite the fact that the message from the Kobe doctor deprived him of transfusions, which would have been the most useful therapy of all, his fever and his digestive troubles cleared up fairly quickly. His white count went up for a while, but early in October it dropped again, to 3,600; then, in ten days, it suddenly climbed above normal, to 8,800; and it finally settled at 5,800. His ridiculous scratches puzzled everyone. For a few days, they would mend, and then, when he moved around, they would open up again. As soon as he began to feel well, he enjoyed himself tremendously. In Hiroshima he had been one of thousands of sufferers; in Tokyo he was a curiosity. Young American Army doctors came by the dozen to observe him. Japanese experts questioned him. A newspaper interviewed him. And once, the confused doctor came and shook his head and said, "Baffling cases, these atomic-bomb people."

Mrs. Nakamura lay indoors with Myeko. They both continued sick, and though Mrs. Nakamura vaguely sensed that their trouble was caused by the bomb, she was too poor to see a doctor and so never knew exactly what the matter was. Without any treatment at all, but merely resting, they began gradually to feel better. Some of Myeko's hair fell out, and she had a tiny burn on her arm which took months to heal. The boy, Toshio, and the older girl, Yaeko, seemed well enough, though they, too, lost some hair and occasionally had bad headaches. Toshio was still having nightmares, always about the nineteen-year-old mechanic, Hideo Osaki, his hero, who had been killed by the bomb.

On his back with a fever of 104, Mr. Tanimoto worried about all the funerals he ought to be conducting for the deceased of his church. He thought he was just overtired from the hard work he had done since the bombing, but after the fever had persisted for a few days, he sent for a doctor. The doctor was too busy to visit him in Ushida, but he dispatched a nurse, who recognized his symptoms as those of mild radiation disease and came back from time to time to give him injections of Vitamin B. A Buddhist priest with whom Mr. Tanimoto was acquainted called on him and suggested that moxibustion might give him relief; the priest showed the pastor how to give himself the ancient Japanese treatment, by setting fire to a twist of the stimulant herb moxa placed on the wrist pulse. Mr. Tanimoto found that each moxa treatment temporarily reduced his fever one degree. The nurse had told him to eat as much as possible, and every few days his mother-in-law brought him vegetables and fish from Tsuzu, twenty miles away, where she lived. He spent a month in bed, and then went ten hours by train to his father's home in Shikoku. There he rested another month.

Dr. Sasaki and his colleagues at the Red Cross Hospital watched the unprecedented disease unfold and at last evolved a theory about its nature. It had, they decided, three stages. The first stage had been all over before the doctors even knew they were dealing with a new sickness; it was the direct reaction to the bombardment of the body, at the moment when the bomb went off, by neutrons, beta particles, and gamma rays. The apparently uninjured people who had died so mysteriously in the first few hours or days had succumbed in this first stage. It killed ninety-five per cent. of the people within a half mile of the centre, and many thousands who were farther away. The doctors realized in retrospect that even though most of these dead had also suffered from burns and blast effects, they had absorbed enough radiation to kill them. The rays simply destroyed body cells—caused their nuclei to degenerate and broke their walls. Many people who did not die right away came down with nausea, headache, diarrhoea, malaise, and fever, which lasted several days. Doctors could not be certain whether some of these symptoms were the result of radiation or nervous shock. The second stage set in ten or fifteen days after the bombing. The main symptom was falling hair. Diarrhoea and fever, which in some cases went as high as 106, came next. Twenty-five to thirty days after the explosion, blood disorders appeared: gums bled, the white-blood-cell count dropped sharply, and *petechiae* appeared on the skin and mucous membranes. The drop in the number of white blood corpuscles reduced the patient's capacity to resist infection, so open wounds were unusually slow in healing and many of the sick developed sore throats and mouths. The two key symptoms, on which the doctors came to base their prognosis, were fever and the lowered white-corpuscle count. If fever remained steady and high, the patient's chances for survival were poor. The white count almost always dropped below four thousand; a patient whose count fell below one thousand had little hope of living. Toward the end of the second stage, if the patient survived, anaemia, or a drop in the red blood count, also set in. The third stage was the reaction that came when the body struggled to compensate for its ills— when, for instance, the white count not only returned to normal but increased to much higher than normal levels. In this stage, many patients died of complications, such as infections in the chest cavity. Most burns healed with deep layers of pink, rubbery scar tissue, known as keloid tumours. The duration of the disease varied, depending on the patient's constitution and the amount of radiation he had received. Some victims recovered in a week; with others the disease dragged on for months.

As the symptoms revealed themselves, it became clear that many of them resembled the effects of over-doses of X-ray, and the doctors based their therapy on that likeness. They gave victims liver extract, blood transfusions, and vitamins, especially B_1. The shortage of supplies and instruments hampered them. Allied doctors who came in after the surrender found plasma and penicillin very effective. Since the blood disorders were, in the long run, the predominant factor in the disease, some of the Japanese doctors evolved a theory as to the seat of the delayed sickness. They thought that perhaps gamma rays, entering the body at the time of the explosion, made the phosphorus in the victims' bones radio-active, and that they in turn emitted beta particles, which, though they could not penetrate far through flesh, could enter the bone marrow, where blood is manufactured, and gradually tear it down. Whatever its source, the disease had some baffling quirks. Not all the patients exhibited all the main symptoms. People who suffered flash burns were protected, to a considerable extent, from radiation sickness. Those who had lain quietly for days or even hours after the bombing were much less liable to get sick than those who had been active. Grey hair seldom fell out. And, as if nature were protecting man against his own ingenuity, the reproductive processes were affected for a time; men became sterile, women had miscarriages, menstruation stopped.

For ten days after the flood, Dr. Fujii lived in the peasant's house on the mountain above the Ota. Then he heard about a vacant private clinic in Kaitaichi, a suburb to the east of Hiroshima. He bought it at once, moved there, and hung out a sign inscribed in English, in honour of the conquerors:

M. Fujii, m.d.

Medical and Venereal

Quite recovered from his wounds, he soon built up

a strong practice, and he was delighted, in the evenings, to receive members of the occupying forces, on whom he lavished whisky and practised English.

Giving Miss Sasaki a local anaesthetic of procaine, Dr. Sasaki made an incision in her leg on October 23rd, to drain the infection, which still lingered on eleven weeks after the injury. In the following days, so much pus formed that he had to dress the opening each morning and evening. A week later, she complained of great pain, so he made another incision; he cut still a third, on November 9th, and enlarged it on the twenty-sixth. All this time, Miss Sasaki grew, weaker and weaker, and her spirits fell low. One day, the young man who had lent her his translation of de Maupassant at Hatsukaichi came to visit her; he told her that he was going to Kyushu but that when he came back, he would like to see her again. She didn't care. Her leg had been so swollen and painful all along that the doctor had not even tried to set the fractures, and though an X-ray taken in November showed that the bones were mending, she could see under the sheet that her left leg was nearly three inches shorter than her right and that her left foot was turning inward. She thought often of the man to whom she had been engaged. Someone told her he was back from overseas. She wondered what he had heard about her injuries that made him stay away.

Father Kleinsorge was discharged from the hospital in Tokyo on December 19th and took a train home. On the way, two days later, at Yokogawa, a stop just before Hiroshima, Dr. Fujii boarded the train. It was the first time the two men had met since before the bombing. They sat together. Dr. Fujii said he was going to the annual gathering of his family, on the anniversary of his father's death. When they started talking about their experiences, the Doctor was quite entertaining as he told how his places of residence kept falling into rivers. Then he asked Father Kleinsorge how he was, and the Jesuit talked about his stay in the hospital. "The doctors told me to be cautious," he said. "They ordered me to have a two-hour nap every afternoon."

Dr. Fujii said, "It's hard to be cautious in Hiroshima these days. Everyone seems to be so busy."

A new municipal government, set up under Allied Military Government direction, had gone to work at last in the city hall. Citizens who had recovered from various degrees of radiation sickness were coming back by the thousand—by November 1st, the population, mostly crowded into the outskirts, was already 137,000, more than a third of the war-time peak—and the government set in motion all kinds of projects to put them to work rebuilding the city. It hired men to clear the streets, and others to gather scrap iron, which they sorted and piled in mountains opposite the city hall. Some returning residents were putting up their own shanties and huts, and planting small squares of winter wheat beside them, but the city also authorised and built four hundred one-family "barracks." Utilities were repaired—electric lights shone again, trams started running, and employees of the waterworks fixed seventy thousand leaks in mains and plumbing. A Planning Conference, with an enthusiastic young Military Government officer,

Lieutenant John D. Montgomery, of Kalamazoo, as its adviser, began to consider what sort of city the new Hiroshima should be. The ruined city had flourished—and had been an inviting target—mainly because it had been one of the most important military-command and communications centres in Japan, and would have become the Imperial headquarters had the islands been invaded and Tokyo been captured. Now there would be no huge military establishments to help revive the city. The Planning Conference, at a loss as to just what importance Hiroshima could have, fell back on rather vague cultural and paving projects. It drew maps with avenues a hundred yards wide and thought seriously of preserving the half-ruined Museum of Science and Industry more or less as it was, as a monument to the disaster, and naming it the Institute of International Amity. Statistical workers gathered what figures they could on the effects of the bomb. They reported that 78,150 people had been killed, 13,983 were missing, and 37,425 had been injured. No one in the city government pretended that these figures were accurate—though the Americans accepted them as official—and as the months went by and more and more hundreds of corpses were dug up from the ruins, and as the number of unclaimed urns of ashes at the Zempoji Temple in Koi rose into the thousands, the statisticians began to say that at least a hundred thousand people had lost their lives in the bombing. Since many people died of a combination of causes, it was impossible to figure exactly how many were killed by each cause, but the statisticians calculated that about twenty-five per cent. had died of

direct burns from the bomb, about fifty per cent. from
other injuries, and about twenty per cent. as a result
of radiation effects. The statisticians' figures on
property damage were more reliable: sixty-two thousand out of ninety thousand buildings destroyed,
and six thousand more damaged beyond repair. In the
heart of the city, they found only five modern
buildings that could be used again without major
repairs. This small number was by no means the fault
of flimsy Japanese construction. In fact, since the
1923 earthquake, Japanese building regulations had
required that the roof of each large building be
able to bear a minimum load of seventy pounds per
square foot, whereas American regulations do not
normally specify more than forty pounds per square
foot.

Scientists swarmed into the city. Some of them
measured the force that had been necessary to shift
marble gravestones in the cemeteries, to knock over
twenty-two of the forty-seven railroad cars in the
yards at Hiroshima station, to lift and move the
concrete roadway on one of the bridges, and to perform
other noteworthy acts of strength, and concluded that
the pressure exerted by the explosion varied from 5.3
to 8.0 tons per square yard. Others found that mica,
of which the melting point is 900° C., had fused on
granite gravestones three hundred and eighty yards
from the centre; that telephone poles of *Cryptomeria
japonica*, whose carbonisation temperature is 240° C.,
had been charred at forty-four hundred yards from
the centre; and that the surface of grey clay tiles of
the type used in Hiroshima. whose melting point is

1,300° C., had dissolved at six hundred yards; and after examining other significant ashes and melted bits, they concluded that the bomb's heat on the ground at the centre must have been 6,000° C. And from further measurements of radiation, which involved, among other things, the scraping up of fission fragments from roof troughs and drainpipes as far away as the suburb of Takasu, thirty-three hundred yards from the centre, they learned some far more important facts about the nature of the bomb. General MacArthur's headquarters systematically censored all mention of the bomb in Japanese scientific publications, but soon the fruit of the scientists' calculations became common knowledge among Japanese physicists, doctors, chemists, journalists, professors, and, no doubt, those statesmen and military men who were still in circulation. Long before the American public had been told, most of the scientists and lots of non-scientists in Japan knew—from the calculations of Japanese nuclear physicists—that a uranium bomb had exploded at Hiroshima and a more powerful one, of plutonium, at Nagasaki. They also knew that theoretically one ten times as powerful—or twenty—could be developed. The Japanese scientists thought they knew the exact height at which the bomb at Hiroshima was exploded and the approximate weight of the uranium used. They estimated that, even with the primitive bomb used at Hiroshima, it would require a shelter of concrete fifty inches thick to protect a human being entirely from radiation sickness. The scientists had these and other details which remained subject to security in the United States printed and mimeographed and bound into little books. The Americans knew of the existence of these, but tracing them and seeing that they did not fall into the wrong hands would have obliged the occupying authorities to set up, for this one purpose alone, an enormous police system in Japan. Altogether, the Japanese scientists were somewhat amused at the efforts of their conquerors to keep security on atomic fission.

Late in February, 1946, a friend of Miss Sasaki's called on Father Kleinsorge and asked him to visit her in the hospital. She had been growing more and more depressed and morbid; she seemed little interested in living. Father Kleinsorge went to see her several times. On his first visit, he kept the conversation general, formal, and yet vaguely sympathetic, and did not mention religion. Miss Sasaki herself brought it up the second time he dropped in on her. Evidently she had had some talks with a Catholic. She asked bluntly, "If your God is so good and kind, how can he let people 'suffer like this?" She made a gesture which took in her shrunken leg, the other patients in her room, and Hiroshima as a whole.

"My child," Father Kleinsorge said, "man is not now in the condition God intended. He has fallen from grace through sin." And he went on to explain all the reasons for everything.

It came to Mrs. Nakamura's attention that a carpenter from Kabe was building a number of wooden shanties in Hiroshima which he rented for fifty yen a month—$3.33, at the fixed rate of exchange. Mrs. Nakamura had lost the certificates for her bonds and other wartime savings, but fortunately she had copied

off all the numbers just a few days before the bombing
and had taken the list to Kabe, and so, when her hair
had grown in enough for her to be presentable, she
went to her bank in Hiroshima, and a clerk there
told her that after checking her numbers against the
records the bank would give her her money. As soon as
she got it, she rented one of the carpenter's shacks.
It was in Nobori-cho, near the site of her former house,
and though its floor was dirt and it was dark inside,
it was at least a home in Hiroshima, and she was no
longer dependent on the charity of her in-laws. During
the spring, she cleared away some nearby wreckage
and planted a vegetable garden. She cooked with
utensils and ate off plates she scavenged from the
debris. She sent Myeko to the kindergarten which the
Jesuits reopened, and the two older children attended
Nobori-cho Primary School, which, for want of
buildings, held classes out of doors. Toshio wanted
to study to be a mechanic, like his hero, Hideo Osaki.
Prices were high; by midsummer Mrs. Nakamura's
savings were gone. She sold some of her clothes
to get food. She had once had several expensive
kimonos, but during the war one had been stolen,
she had given one to a sister who had been bombed
out in Tokuyama, she had lost a couple in the Hiroshima bombing, and now she sold her last one. It
brought only a hundred yen, which did not last long.
In June, she went to Father Kleinsorge for advice
about how to get along, and in early August, she was
still considering the two alternatives he suggested—
taking work as a domestic for some of the Allied
occupation forces, or borrowing from her relatives

enough money, about five hundred yen, or a bit more than thirty dollars, to repair her rusty sewing machine and resume the work of a seamstress.

When Mr. Tanimoto returned from Shikoku, he draped a tent he owned over the roof of the badly damaged house he had rented in Ushida. The roof still leaked, but he conducted services in the damp living-room. He began thinking about raising money to restore his church in the city. He became quite friendly with Father Kleinsorge and saw the Jesuits often. He envied them their Church's wealth; they seemed to be able to do anything they wanted. He had nothing to work with except his own energy, and that was not what it had been.

The Society of Jesus had been the first institution to build a relatively permanent shanty in the ruins of Hiroshima. That had been while Father Kleinsorge was in the hospital. As soon as he got back, he began living in the shack, and he and another priest, Father Laderman, who had joined him in the mission, arranged for the purchase of three of the standardised " barracks," which the city was selling at seven thousand yen apiece. They put two together, end to end, and made a pretty chapel of them; they ate in the third. When materials were available, they commissioned a contractor to build a three-storey mission house exactly like the one that had been destroyed in the fire. In the compound, carpenters cut timbers, gouged mortises, shaped tenons, whittled scores of wooden pegs and bored holes for them, until all the parts for the house were in a neat pile; then, in three days, they put the whole thing together,

like an Oriental puzzle, without any nails at all. Father
Kleinsorge was finding it hard, as Dr. Fujii had
suggested he would,. to be cautious and to take his
naps. He went out every day on foot to call on
Japanese Catholics and prospective converts. As the
months went by, he grew more and more tired. In
June, he read an article in the Hiroshima *Chugoku*
warning survivors against working too hard—but
what could he do? By July, he was worn out, and
early in August, almost exactly on the anniversary of
the bombing, he went back to the Catholic International Hospital, in Tokyo, for a month's rest.

Whether or not Father Kleinsorge's answers to Miss
Sasaki's questions about life were final and absolute
truths, she seemed quickly to draw physical strength
from them. Dr. Sasaki noticed it and congratulated
Father Kleinsorge. By April 15th, her temperature
and white count were normal and the infection in the
wound was beginning to clear up. On the twentieth,
there was almost no pus, and for the first time she
jerked along a corridor on crutches. Five days later,
the wound had begun to heal, and on the last day of
the month she was discharged.

During the early summer, she prepared herself for
conversion to Catholicism. In that period she had
ups and downs. Her depressions were deep. She
knew she would always be a cripple. Her fiancé
never came to see her. There was nothing for her
to do except read and look out, from her house on a
hillside in Koi, across the ruins of the city where her
parents and brother died. She was nervous, and any
sudden noise made her put her hands quickly to her

throat. Her leg still hurt; she rubbed it often and patted it, as if to console it.

It took six months for the Red Cross Hospital, and even longer for Dr. Sasaki to get back to normal. Until the city restored electric power, the hospital had to limp along with the aid of a Japanese Army generator in its back yard. Operating tables, X-ray machines, dentist chairs, everything complicated and essential came in a trickle of charity from other cities. In Japan, face is important even to institutions, and long before the Red Cross Hospital was back to par on basic medical equipment, its directors put up a new yellow brick veneer façade, so the hospital became the handsomest building in Hiroshima—from the street. For the first four months, Dr. Sasaki was the only surgeon on the staff and he almost never left the building; then, gradually, he began to take an interest in his own life again. He got married in March. He gained back some of the weight he lost, but his appetite remained only fair; before the bombing, he used to eat four rice balls at every meal, but a year after it he could manage only two. He felt tired all the time. "But I have to realise," he said, "that the whole community is tired."

A year after the bomb was dropped, Miss Sasaki was a cripple; Mrs. Nakamura was destitute; Father Kleinsorge was back in the hospital; Dr. Sasaki was not capable of the work he once could do; Dr. Fujii had lost the thirty-room hospital it took him many years to acquire, and had no prospects of rebuilding it; Mr. Tanimoto's church had been ruined and he no longer had his exceptional vitality. The lives of these six people, who were among the luckiest in Hiroshima, would never be the same. What they thought of their experiences and the use of the atomic bomb was, of course, not unanimous. One feeling they did seem to share, however, was a curious kind of elated community spirit, something like that of the Londoners after their blitz—a pride in the way they and their fellow-survivors had stood up to a dreadful ordeal. Just before the anniversary, Mr. Tanimoto wrote in a letter to an American some words which expressed this feeling: "What a heartbreaking scene this was the first night ! About midnight I landed on the river-bank. So many injured people lay on the ground that I made my way by striding over them. Repeating "Excuse me," I forwarded and carried a tub of water with me and gave a cup of water to each one of them. They raised their upper bodies slowly and accepted a cup of water with a bow and drunk quietly and, spilling any remnant, gave back a cup with hearty expression of their thankfulness, and said, ' I couldn't help my sister, who was buried under the house, because I had to take care of my mother who got a deep wound on her eye and our house soon set fire and we hardly escaped. Look, I lost my home, my family, and at last myself bitterly injured. But now I have got my mind to dedicate what I have and to complete the war for our country's sake.' Thus they pledged to me, even women and children did the same. Being entirely tired I lied down on the ground among them, but couldn't sleep at all. Next morning I found many men and women dead, whom I gave water last night   But, to my great surprise, I never heard any one cry in disorder, even though they suffered in great agony. They died in silence, with no grudge, setting their teeth to bear it. All for the country !

" Dr. Y. Hiraiwa, professor of Hiroshima University of Literature and Science, and one of my church members, was buried by the bomb under the two-storied house with his son, a student of Tokyo University. Both of them could not move an inch under tremendously heavy pressure. And the house already caught fire. His son said, ' Father, we can do nothing, except make our mind up to consecrate our lives for the country. Let us give *Banzai* to our Emperor.' Then the father followed after his son, ' *Tenno-heika, Banzai, Banzai, Banzai !* ' In the result, Dr. Hiraiwa said, ' Strange to say, I felt calm and bright and peaceful spirit in my heart, when I chanted *Banzai* to Tènno.' Afterwards his son got out and digged down and pulled out his father and thus they were saved. In thinking of their experience of that time Dr. Hiraiwa repeated, ' What a fortunate that we are Japanese ! It was my first time I ever tasted such a beautiful spirit when I decided to die for our Emperor.'

" Miss Kayoko Nobutoki, a student of girl's high school, Hiroshima Jazabuin, and a daughter of my church member, was taking rest with her friends beside the heavy fence of the Buddhist Temple. At the moment the atomic bomb was dropped, the fence fell upon them. They could not move a bit under such a heavy fence and then smoke entered into even a crack and choked their breath. One of the girls begun to sing *Kimi ga yo*, national anthem, and others followed in chorus and died. Meanwhile one of them found a crack and struggled hard to get out. When she was taken in the Red Cross Hospital she told how her friends died, tracing back in her memory to singing in chorus our national anthem. They were just thirteen years old.

" Yes, people of Hiroshima died manly in the atomic bombing, believing that it was for Emperor's sake."

A surprising number of the people of Hiroshima remained more or less indifferent about the ethics of using the bomb. Possibly they were too terrified by it to want to think about it at all. Not many of them even bothered to find out much about what it was like. Mrs. Nakamura's conception of it—and awe of it— was typical. " The atom bomb," she would say when asked about it, " is the size of a matchbox. The heat of it was six thousand times that of the sun. It exploded in the air. There is some radium in it. I don't know just how it works, but when the radium is put together, it explodes." As for the use of the bomb, she would say, " It was war and we had to expect it." And then she would add, " *Shikata ga nai*," a Japanese expression as common as, and corresponding to, the Russian word " *nichevo* " : " It can't be helped. Oh, well. Too bad." Dr. Fujii said approximately the same thing about the use of the bomb to Father Kleinsorge one evening, in German : " *Da ist nichts zu machen*. There's nothing to be done about it."

Many citizens of Hiroshima, however, continued to feel a hatred for Americans which nothing could possibly erase. "I see," Dr. Sasaki once said, "that they are holding a trial for war criminals in Tokyo just now. I think they ought to try the men who decided to use the bomb and they should hang them all."

Father Kleinsorge and the other German Jesuit priests, who, as foreigners, could be expected to take a relatively detached view, often discussed the ethics of using the bomb. One of them, Father Siemes, who was out at Nagatsuka at the time of the attack, wrote in a report to the Holy See in Rome, "Some of us consider the bomb in the same category as poison gas and were against its use on a civilian population. Others were of the opinion that in total war, as carried on in Japan, there was no difference between civilians and soldiers, and that the bomb itself was an effective force tending to end the bloodshed, warning Japan to surrender and thus to avoid total destruction. It seems logical that he who supports total war in principle cannot complain of a war against civilians. The crux of the matter is whether total war in its present form is justifiable, even when it serves a just purpose. Does it not have material and spiritual evil as its consequences which far exceed whatever good might result? When will our moralists give us a clear answer to this question?"

It would be impossible to say what horrors were embedded in the minds of the children who lived through the day of the bombing in Hiroshima. On the surface their recollections, months after the disaster, were of an exhilarating adventure. Toshio Nakamura, who was ten at the time of the bombing, was soon able to talk freely, even gaily, about the experience, and a few weeks before the anniversary he wrote the following matter-of-fact essay for his teacher at Nobori-cho Primary School: " The day before the bomb, I went for a swim. In the morning, I was eating peanuts. I saw a light. I was knocked to little sister's sleeping place. When we were saved I could only see as far as the tram. My mother and I started to pack our things. The neighbours were walking around burned and bleeding. Hataya-*san* told me to run away with her. I said I wanted to wait for my mother. We went to the park. A whirlwind came. At night a gas tank burned and I saw the reflection in the river. We stayed in the park one night. Next day I went to Taiko Bridge and met my girl friends Kikuki and Murakami. They were looking for their mothers. But Kikuki's mother was wounded and Murakami's mother, alas, was dead."

Get Published!

"Everyone has something they know well or can do well. And when a person has a skill, there's always going to be someone willing to pay for it."

— *bnpublishing.com*

BN Publishing helps authors publish more titles. So whether you're writing a romance novel, a historical fiction, a mystery, action or suspense story, poetry, about business, a children's book, or any other, we can help you reach your publishing goals.

Besides telling a story, a book is a promotional tool. A book can be likened to a powerful business card since most people won't throw it out. Authoring a book can give you credibility and status, enabling you to charge more for your services.
With our best resources, we will help expose your talent to the public and publish your book for FREE!

Your writing will reach 20,000 retail accounts in the United States (chains, independents, specialty stores, and libraries), including:

www.amazon.com

www.amazon.co.uk

www.amazon.ca

www.bn.com

www.powells.com

www.ebay.com

and more...

Your book will be also included in a physical catalog which goes out to retail stores. Furthermore, when your title is entered into our library, it will automatically appear in bookstore and library databases.

Our United States- and United Kingdom-based sales teams work with clients all over the world through our broad distribution channel partners.

For more information please contact

editor@bnpublishing.net

Recommended Readings

nk and Grow Rich by Napoleon Hill

e Master-Key to Riches by Napoleon Hill

e Law of Success In Sixteen Lessons (Complete, Unabridged) (2 Disc Set) by ɔoleon Hill

rren Buffett Talks to MBA Students by Warren Buffett

e General Theory of Employment, Interest, and Money by John Maynard ʏnes

w I Learned the Secrets of Success in Selling by Frank Bettger

ı Can Still Make It In The Market by Nicolas Darvas

e Richest Man in Babylon - Illustrated by George S. Clason

est like a Billionaire: If you are not watching the best investor in the world, ɔ are you watching?

ɔw Me Your Options! The Guide to Complete Confidence for Every Stock and tions Trader Seeking Consistent, Predictable Returns
Steve Burns, Christopher Ebert

ɔk to School: Question & Answer Session with Business Students by Warren ffett

w Trader, Rich Trader: How to Make Money in the Stock Market by Steve ɾns

Available at   www.bnpublishing.com

CPSIA information can be obtained
at www.ICGtesting.com
Printed in the USA
BVHW031539230820
587089BV00010B/40